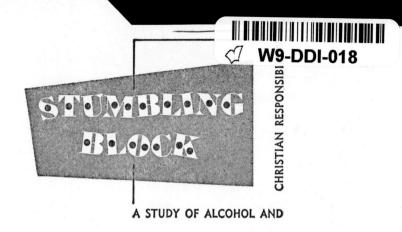

STUMBLING BLOCK

A STUDY OF ALCOHOL AND CHRISTIAN RESPONSIBILITY

by

Douglas Jackson

with an introduction by

Bishop Arthur J. Moore

Published by

EDITORIAL DEPARTMENT
Joint Section of Education and Cultivation
Board of Missions of The Methodist Church
475 Riverside Drive, New York 27, N.Y.

STUMBLING BLOCK

10-4-00

Approved as a text for the

LEADERSHIP EDUCATION PROGRAM

General Board of Education of The Methodist Church

Library of Congress Number 60-9819

SECOND EDITION

1478(rv1355)-MPH   11-60-40M (115th M)

Set up, printed and bound by The Parthenon Press, Nashville, Tennessee, U.S.A.

Contents

TO MY PARENTS

NO HONEST and intelligent person can deny that throughout these United States of America we are face to face with a beverage alcohol problem of incredible magnitude. We are compelled as Christians and citizens of our nation to look clear-eyed at this evil thing and to devise ways and means whereby the organized traffic can be restrained and ultimately destroyed. This will demand a sustained program of temperance education by which our people, adults and youth alike, learn how to meet this social evil with convictions and stout courage.

Here is an issue with which Methodists have been concerned from the beginning, and indeed it is a problem that the New Testament Church faced long before the advent of fortified wines, distilled spirits, high-speed motor cars, psychoanalysis, and atomic wars. The "noble experiment" with national prohibition was largely the result of many years of education and action by Protestant Christians. Sobriety, abstinence from intoxicants, and a sense of concern for broken hearts and broken homes and broken lives are still marks of a dedicated Methodist. It is the purpose of this book to give us a clearer understanding of what is required of sincere churchmen and to provide the new approach the times demand.

This problem of alcohol is also a world problem. In many lands, as in our own, many of those to whom the gospel comes as a liberating and life-changing message are among those who suffer directly or indirectly from the effects of the use and sale of alcoholic beverages. The problem has a crucial bearing upon all our mission work at home and overseas. In the home field, the use and abuse of intoxicating beverages contributes to every difficulty we meet. The five million alcoholics across the land constitute in themselves a vast and demanding area of spiritual need. The added millions of problem drinkers are a challenge to our moral, spiritual, and economic resources, and these millions need our understanding and help.

It is the considered opinion of many of those in places of responsibility for the promotion and administration of our missionary program that this study is not only in proper place, but that it is of basic importance for the whole mission of the church. The author has given us, in language all can understand, an objective and dispassionate appraisal, from the adult point of view, of alcohol and alcoholism in our day. It is an appeal to common sense and Christian responsibility. It is a study which will help every churchman who reads it face more intelligently and honestly this problem which affects our homes, our church and the strength of our beloved country.

We are indebted to Dr. Douglas Jackson for a clear and careful analysis of the problem. Simplicity of style, careful marshalling of facts, and swift movement of thought will make reading a pleasure. It is hoped that Methodists everywhere will find in this excellent and effective approach a call "To solve with skill and grace the problems of intoxicants and to crash this formidable barrier."

ARTHUR J. MOORE

Atlanta, Georgia
February 22, 1960

CHAPTER I

What Alcohol Is and Does

ALCOHOL has been used as a beverage from the earliest periods of history. One brewing company has recited the use of beer by the Puritan colonists. Another has assured us that "beer belongs." Certainly man has been using alcoholic beverages for centuries.

Man discovered alcoholic beverages through the natural fermentation of fruit juices and grains. Most ancient tribes used some form of fermented drink. Certain non-agricultural tribes, however, did not use alcohol. Included among these tribes were the Polar peoples, Australian bushmen, and many of the American Indian tribes. The early traders and explorers introduced the use of alcohol to these tribes.

FERMENTATION

Natural fermentation of any fruit juice produces wine. Fruit sugar, or glucose, is present in every fruit juice. Unless fruit juice is boiled or cooled, it will ferment. Yeast naturally present in the juice or in the air reacts chemically with the glucose to produce alcohol. Fermentation ceases when the alcohol content of the wine reaches about 14 per cent.

Grapes are most commonly used in the production of wine. Berries and other fruits were more commonly used in the ancient world than currently.

Fermentation of grains or vegetables produces beer. Any starchy food such as corn, wheat, rye, rice, or potatoes can be used to produce beer. Malt added to the mashed substance changes the starch to sugar. Fermentation of the sugar then occurs in a manner similar to the fermentation which occurs in the production of wine.

Fermentation of beer usually ceases when the alcohol content of the brew reaches 3 to 6 per cent. The usual alcohol content of American beer is about 4 per cent. Hops are added to the beer for flavor.

Ale, another type of brew, is more commonly used in Britain than in this country. Usually ale contains no hops. Ale may also have a slightly higher alcoholic content than beer.

Fermentation is a relatively simple process. Wines, beers, and ales were, therefore, readily available to many ancient peoples. These low alcoholic content beverages were often valued as food or medicines. These beverages seemed to relieve fatigue.

The low-alcoholic-content wines and beers are capable of producing intoxication. Ancient writings carry warnings against drunkenness. Various writings in the Old Testament indicate that the Hebrews recognized the dangers of drinking intoxicants.

Noah, Lot, and Nabal are pictured as prominent men who brought great troubles upon themselves because of drunkenness. King Lemuel is advised not to drink wine lest he fail in his duties as a king. Isaiah pronounces a judgment upon drunkenness: "Woe to those who rise early in the morning, that they may run after strong drink, who tarry late into the evening till wine inflames them" (Isaiah 5:11). Strong drink produces muddled thinking (Isaiah 28:7), uncontrolled speech (Proverbs 20:1), immodesty (Habakkuk 2:15-16), and physical infirmities (Hosea 7:5).

Many ancient peoples worshiped and appeased their gods through fertility cults. Drunken orgies constituted part of the rites of many of these religions. The Hebrew prophets, noting the cultic rites of the Palestinian religions, condemned the fertility cults and their practices. Drunkenness was condemned as a sin.

DISTILLATION

Despite the many words against drunkenness in the Bible,

only low-alcoholic content beverages were known during the Bible times. Distilled beverages were not commonly available until much later. Distillation was discovered by ancient Greeks and Chinese, but the knowledge was not put to use. Arabs discovered the process and introduced it into Europe during the Middle Ages. Distilled beverages did not become widely available in Europe until the beginning of the sixteenth century.

Distillation is a process which separates liquids having different boiling points. Alcohol boils at a lower temperature than water. Alcohol is distilled by heating wines or beers to a temperature above the boiling point of alcohol. The alcohol becomes a vapor, is conducted through pipes to a condensation chamber, and then reverts to the liquid state. By this process pure alcohol can be distilled.

Brandies, whiskeys, rum, gins, cordials, and liqueurs are dis-

ALCOHOLIC CONTENT OF DRINKS COMPARED

 BEER 4%

 WINE 15%

 WHISKEY 44%

tilled beverages. The alcoholic content of these beverages is usually in the range of 40 to 50 per cent.

The alcoholic content of distilled beverages is usually indicated in terms of proof. Liquor which is classified as 100 proof is 50 per cent alcohol.

Wine is distilled to produce brandy, ranging in strength from 70 proof to 110 proof (35 to 55 per cent alcohol). Whiskeys are distilled from various brews made from grain; whiskeys usually are 85 to 100 proof. Rum is distilled from sugar cane or molasses. Gin is created by steeping juniper berries in diluted alcohol. Cordials and liqueurs are made by adding flavors to diluted alcohol.

The numerous manufacturers of alcoholic beverages produce many brands of drinks. They vary the flavoring, the aging process, and the alcoholic content. The wide range of products is presented in such a fashion as to stimulate sales by appealing to human desires for new experience (variety) and satisfaction of physical desires (taste).

Flavor may play some part in a person's choice of drinks. Most persons, however, do not drink because of taste. One large distiller engaged in research seeking new tastes to prevent his whiskeys from tasting like whiskey; it was recognized that most drinkers did not like the taste of whiskey. Attempts were made to devise alcohol drinks with bizarre tastes—such as banana.

EFFECTS OF ALCOHOL

McCarthy and Douglass have noted: "Near-beer, that is, beer having less than 0.5 per cent alcohol *, has never been popular although it has excellent flavor and thirst-quenching qualities. . . . On the whole, the popularity of brewed, fermented, and distilled beverages over the centuries is accounted for primarily

---

*Notice that "0.5 per cent" is to be read, "five tenths of 1 per cent" (not "5 per cent"). Similarly in following paragraphs observe that "0.15 per cent" is to be read "fifteen one-hundredths of 1 per cent," etc. Beverages of 0.5 per cent alcohol have one part alcohol in two hundred parts of liquid.

by the presence of alcohol in the drink and by the effect of alcohol on the drinker." [1]

The flavor of wines and beers is not enough to satisfy many drinkers. Fermented drinks are often "fortified" with additional alcohol. Fortified wines have distilled alcohol added to bring the alcohol content up to 20 per cent.

The alcohol in beverages produces significant effects only after it is absorbed into the blood. Alcohol does not require digestion but may pass rapidly into the blood stream from the stomach and small intestine.

The rate of absorption of alcohol by the blood is affected by many factors. The rate can vary according to the type of drink, its alcoholic content, the contents of the stomach, the speed of drinking, and individual constitutional factors. Alcohol taken on an empty stomach is absorbed very rapidly, with 30 to 40 per cent passing directly from the stomach into the blood stream. The other alcohol passes quickly into the intestine and is absorbed at a rapid rate. Alcohol may be detected in the blood within five minutes after consumption upon an empty stomach.

The rate of absorption of alcohol is directly affected by the amount and type of food present in the stomach at the time of the drinking. The type of beverage also affects the rate of absorption. Brewed beverages usually contain food materials such as carbohydrates and proteins which slow up absorption.

Although the rate of absorption is relatively constant for everyone, large persons are less rapidly affected by alcohol. The greater amounts of blood and body fluids in the large person dilute the alcohol and lessen its effects.

The effects of alcohol can be rather accurately gauged by the concentration of alcohol in the blood. There is no discernible effect upon behavior as long as the concentration of alcohol in the blood does not exceed 0.05 per cent (5 parts of alcohol in 10,000 parts of blood). Alcohol begins to affect persons at a

[1] Raymond G. McCarthy and Edgar M. Douglass, *Alcohol and Social Responsibility: A New Educational Approach,* New York: Thomas Y. Crowell Company and Yale Plan Clinic, 1949, p. 88.

concentration of 0.05 per cent, but some persons appear unaffected at a concentration up to 0.15 per cent. With a concentration between 0.05 and 0.15 per cent most persons are affected in speech and movement. When the alcohol content passes 0.15 per cent the effect can no longer be concealed; intoxication is definitely established. These standards for definition of intoxication have been established in law in several states.

When the concentration of alcohol in the blood reaches a level of 0.4 per cent (40 parts per 10,000), the drinker has usually passed into stupor. At a level of 0.5 per cent the drinker is in danger of dying due to deep anesthesia.

The concentration of alcohol in the blood is determined by the rate of absorption, elimination, and oxidation. The rate of absorption is dependent upon the factors of speed of drinking, type of drinks, and bodily condition. The rate of elimination and oxidation is relatively fixed and unaffected by the pattern of drinking.

Small amounts of alcohol are eliminated from the body through the kidneys, the lungs, and the salivary glands. Approximately 80 to 90 per cent of the alcohol must be disposed of, however, through oxidation. The rate of oxidation is relatively constant and rather slow. Drinking generally builds up the concentration of alcohol in the blood at a rate faster than it can be oxidized. The highest concentration of alcohol in the blood usually occurs within sixty to ninety minutes after drinking.

Within sixty to ninety minutes after the drinking has ceased, the alcohol content in the blood begins to decrease. Several hours must elapse before an alcohol concentration of 0.15 per cent is removed. An intoxicated person with an alcohol concentration of 0.30 per cent will require 12 to 15 hours to "sleep it off."

The major effects of alcohol arise from the concentration of alcohol in the blood. An additional effect that sometimes occurs is the irritation of the throat or the stomach. Irritation of the throat is the more common and requires a beverage with an alcohol content of 15 per cent or more in most cases. The higher the alcohol content, the more likely is irritation.

An alcoholic drink which produces irritation affects the nerve endings in the throat and esophagus. The irritation increases the pulse rate and sometimes raises the blood pressure. Continued irritation of the throat can produce a change in vocal tone. Daily use of large quantities of alcohol can produce continued inflammations of the digestive tract. The burning or smarting effect immediately accompanying a drink of 40 to 50 per cent alcohol is due to the irritating properties of alcohol.

IN THE BLOOD STREAM

The effects of alcohol in the blood stream arise from the anesthetic properties of alcohol. Alcohol is classified by pharmacists as a drug producing progressive depressant action on the central nervous system. Alcohol acts as an anesthetic like ether or chloroform; all are depressants of the central nervous system.

Varying dosages of alcohol can produce the relaxing effect of a sedative, the pain-relieving effect of an analgesic, or the sleep-producing effect of a hypnotic drug. Because of the varying effects of alcohol it has been classified as sedative, analgesic, hypnotic, and narcotic. The most accurate classification, however, is that of anesthetic.

Anesthetic action is generally associated with the unconscious state. Any person in a drunken stupor is as completely anesthetized as a patient made unconscious by ether. In early America alcohol was used as an anesthetic for surgery.

The stupor is produced by the effect of alcohol on the lower brain centers. An excessively high concentration of alcohol will anesthetize the lower brain centers which control involuntary body functions. The concentration of alcohol can become high enough to affect the brain centers controlling breathing. When such a concentration occurs, death by suffocation results. Such deaths are quite uncommon. The usual pattern of drinking produces a stupor before the drinker has opportunity to ingest enough alcohol to produce asphyxiation.

The stupor arising from extreme intoxication is the end result of a continuous action that began with the first concentration of alcohol in the blood. The anesthetic action of alcohol begins with the higher brain centers. Only in the last stages of intoxication are the lower brain centers affected.

The higher brain centers, which are first affected, control the higher intellectual functions. Thought processes involving learning, memory, and evaluation become difficult and exhibit disturbances. The capacity for self-criticism rather quickly disappears. Inhibitions tend to lose their force. The practiced drinker learns to anticipate some of these changes and is able at first to engage in compensatory action which conceals the first effects of alcohol. Outwardly unaffected, he may actually be seriously affected in judgment.

These higher brain centers are definitely affected when the alcohol concentration in the blood reaches the level of 0.05 per cent. There is no escape from the depressant action of alcohol upon the brain. A tolerance for alcohol cannot be created, no matter how long a person practices drinking. A practiced drinker may learn how to slow the concentration of alcohol in the blood (slow drinking when the stomach is filled with food), but he cannot change its effects when it reaches the blood.

As the depressant action of alcohol first affects the higher brain centers, a sense of exhilaration seems to develop. It appears that the drinker has taken a stimulant, but the actual result is a slight anesthetizing of the cortex, the outer layer of gray matter, of the brain. Euphoria develops—a feeling of well-being and loss of care. Social restraints and conscience are dulled. The sedative effect of alcohol incapacitates the brain for the exercise of its highest functions. Speech and laughter flow easily.

When the alcohol content in the blood reaches a concentration of 0.15 per cent, the intoxicating effects are more easily discerned. The depressant effect of the alcohol begins seriously to hamper motor and sensory controls in the brain. Coordination is disturbed, and precise actions become difficult and unpredictable. Poor enunciation and thick speech develop. Muscular movements of all types are upset. Memory and emotional control are frequently affected.

The practiced drinker may conceal a number of the results of drinking, even after his motor and sensory controls have been impaired. He may have learned that he must refrain from certain patterns of action since he is unable to control these actions. But often he does not refrain, for example, from driving a motor car. He may even sense a surge of power and competence—a false judgment quite dangerous to himself and to others.

The loss of control proceeds as the rate of alcohol concentration increases. At a blood level of 0.2 per cent the drinker may become markedly offensive. Inhibitions and self-control no longer seem operative. Individuals vary widely, however, in their patterns of action at this level of intoxication. Some become angry and aggressive. Others drop into a deep sleep without regard for their surroundings. Uncontrollable weeping or laughing characterizes the intoxication of others. These are individual variations not easily explained. An individual may engage in different activities on different drinking bouts; his pattern of action at such times is not always predictable.

The various effects of alcohol as listed can be easily documented by reference to physiological data. Most persons in present-day American society can verify the results by observation from common experience.

Few drinkers desire the full range of effects deriving from alcoholic intoxication. Even when intoxication is desired, the milder forms of intoxication are sought in nearly all instances. Usually drinking is undertaken with the expectation that only enough drinks will be consumed to produce the euphoria associated with the soothing action of first-stage drinking.

First-stage drinking seeking this sense of well-being lessens

15

discriminatory powers. The desire to engage in controlled drinking may be changed as the higher intellectual powers and inhibitions are weakened. Intoxication develops as drinking continues beyond the level necessary to produce the effects of first-stage drinking. Intoxication is a direct result of continued, excessive drinking, but it may be an indirect result of the depressant effect of the alcohol consumed in first-stage drinking.

WHY SOME PEOPLE DRINK

Drinking persons advance numerous reasons for their drinking, but few indicate that they desire intoxication. Various reasons are indicated as motives for drinking, but other unrealized motives are involved in the drinking of many persons. Motives are very difficult to judge. Particularly is it difficult to determine the relative weight of different reasons for drinking.

It is highly probable that variations in motivation for drinking are related to drinking patterns. The amount of alcohol consumed, the frequency of drinking, and the social effects of drinking may stem from various motives back of drinking patterns.

It has been often observed that for some groups in our society drinking is part of a cultural pattern. Certain ethnic and religious groups have regularly consumed alcohol in connection with national or religious customs. Long-term usage has invested the drinking pattern with significance exceeding the physical effects of alcohol. The culturally defined mode of drinking becomes related to the maintenance of a "way of life" and group identity.

Cultural and religious motivations for drinking are usually subject to social controls evolved over a long period of time. A rejection of the drinking pattern of the group involves to some degree a rejection of the group and its norms. Contrariwise, a questioning of any other of the values of the group, may also lead to a change in attitudes toward drinking.

Excellent studies have been made of drinking patterns among

Jews and Italians.[2] Among both groups drinking is common. Yet, in each group drunkenness is relatively rare. Religion and eating habits are related to the moderate drinking patterns of the Jews. The whole social structure, particularly the family, exerts great pressure against drunkenness and heavy drinking. Among the Italians, including the immigrants to this country, wine is regarded as a food and is consumed at meals.

The culture is not always able to produce moderate drinking patterns. Over a long period of time drunkenness came to be regarded as normal in Ireland.[3] In Ireland the drinking patterns were associated with and probably derived from a complex system of economic agreements.

A person may drink because his cultural or religious group expects him to drink. Problem drinking rarely occurs in certain of these groups. Cultural expectations in some groups may not regard drunkenness and excessive drinking as problem drinking.

The majority of drinkers in American society are not moved to drink by cultural expectations. Many do drink for social reasons, but these differ from cultural reasons. The social groups whose norms are accepted are less well defined and less stable than the cultural groups.

Social acceptance is a major motive underlying the drinking practices of many Americans. Persons drink to achieve social status or to retain status. The different social classes have different drinking patterns. Many adopt drinking patterns associated with the class to which they wish to belong.[4]

Among those who drink seeking social acceptance are those who do not care for or need alcohol. They may be fluent conversationalists without the added lift of a drink. The idea of

---

[2] Charles R. Snyder, *Alcohol and the Jews: A Cultural Study of Drinking and Sobriety*, Glencoe, Illinois: The Free Press and Yale Center of Alcohol Studies, 1958.

Giorgio Lolli *et al.*, *Alcohol in Italian Culture: Food and Wine in Relation to Sobriety among Italians and Italian Americans*, Glencoe, Illinois: The Free Press and Yale Center of Alcohol Studies, 1958.

[3] Raymond G. McCarthy, ed., *Drinking and Intoxication: Selected Readings in Social Attitudes and Controls*, Glencoe, Illinois: The Free Press and Yale Center of Alcohol Studies, 1959.

[4] Vance Packard, *The Status Seekers*, New York: David McKay Company, 1959, pp. 143-6.

intoxication may be quite repulsive to them. They drink, however, to conform to social custom.

A study of reasons for drinking reported that more persons drank for social reasons than for any other set of reasons.[5] Included among the social reasons reported were: sociability; to keep husband company; on festive occasion; brought up with it; and, as a business courtesy. This study lists a number of individual responses showing the impact of social pressure:

"A young New Yorker, recently discharged from the armed forces: 'Liquor is always sold in the places I frequent. You can't have a soda in a night club. It's just not done.' A Pennsylvania housewife: 'People think you're dead if you don't drink.' A well-to-do professional woman, wife of an architect, New York City: 'I hate to make a fuss about refusing. I don't like to be a poor sport.' A poor, elderly, west-coast farmer: 'Just to be a good fellow. You make people mad if you don't.' ... The wife of a Kansas City service-station attendant: 'Sometimes when we have company, I drink it to be sociable.' A young rural Wisconsin schoolteacher: 'I guess just to be sociable. I don't care for it at all. I just choke it down.' A lineman for the telephone company in a Southern town: 'All of our friends drink, so we drink too.' A young nurse: 'I go to the dance hall, and everybody is drinking; so I just drink too.'"[6]

The "business courtesy" reason may be regarded as either a social or an economic reason. In some business circles today pressure to drink is continuously mounting. The Christmas office party has been the occasion of great pressure toward drinking. Salesmen may find that the expense-account drink is expected by potential customers. The social status of military officers is often conditioned by the cocktail parties given. Some businessmen who do not care for alcohol feel forced to drink and serve drinks.

The previously mentioned study of reasons for drinking indicated that nearly half of the drinkers had individual reasons for

---

[5] McCarthy, *op. cit.*, pp. 232 f.
[6] *Ibid.*, p. 233.

drinking. The list of reasons included under the individual category were: "makes me feel good"; "I like it"; "quenches thirst"; "stimulates appetite"; and "health reasons."

Some of the persons who listed individual drinking reasons felt a need of alcohol to loosen up and relax. They needed alcohol to be sociable—or so they thought. But, these drinkers who drink for individual reasons tend to turn toward solitary drinking. The solitary drinker is not really drinking for social reasons. He has deep-seated psychological needs which he attempts to satisfy by resort to alcohol. He is attempting to escape reality rather than to accept reality.

Social pressures are more important in influence upon women than men. Social frustrations, however, produce individual reasons for women to drink.[7]

---

[7] Packard, *op. cit.*, p. 260.

NUMBER OF DRINKERS AND ABSTAINERS

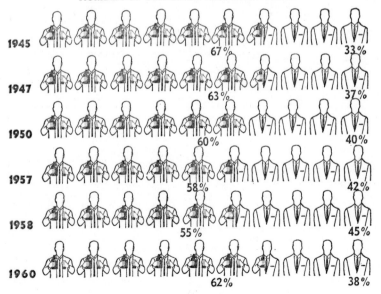

1945	67%	33%
1947	63%	37%
1950	60%	40%
1957	58%	42%
1958	55%	45%
1960	62%	38%

The previously mentioned study also indicated that fewer people drank for social reasons in areas where alcohol was difficult to obtain. Those persons who drank to satisfy individual need were not deterred from drinking by legal reasons. For many social drinkers laws limiting the sale or use of alcohol reduced its use.

Alcohol may be used by some individuals as a medicine or analgesic. Probably not many persons have alcohol recommended by a physician as a medicine, but self-medication still results in the use of various alcoholic potions and beverages. Some well-known patent medicine tonics secure their chief effect from the high alcoholic content.

Alcohol is of limited usefulness as a medicine. Usually only a very small quantity of alcohol is required for medicinal purposes. Some of the diseases of old age are alleviated by the use of alcohol. Some mentally defective persons find in alcohol a partial compensation for their deficiencies.

WHY SOME PEOPLE DO NOT DRINK

Numerous persons in our society do not drink at all. Nearly half the adults in this nation make no use of alcohol whatever. Since 1946 there has been an increase in the proportion of the population who do not drink.[8]

There has been little study of the reasons given for not drinking. A study of reasons given by college and university students lists the following reasons for abstaining from the use of alcohol: "Don't like taste, makes ill, or detrimental to general health; contrary to religious training, immoral, or pledged not to drink; parents or friends disapprove; bad experience of someone else; can't afford it; interferes with participation in sports; friends never use; and, have lost control of drinking in the past."[9]

Religious reasons are generally regarded as most important

[8] Detailed data given in Chapter II, pp. 26-27.
[9] Robert Straus and Selden D. Bacon, *Drinking in College*, New Haven: Yale University Press, 1953, p. 65.

in preventing the use of alcoholic beverages. Various studies have shown that more Protestants abstain from the use of alcohol than do either Roman Catholics or Jews. The Roman Catholic or Jew may use alcohol moderately, as may adherents of some Protestant denominations, but the largest Protestant denominations advocate abstinence.

Sober alcoholics are also abstainers. They can remain sober only so long as they abstain from all use of alcohol.

Since 1946 there has also been a decrease in the amount of alcohol consumed in this nation. The amount spent on alcohol has remained high, but the price of alcohol has risen during the period since 1946. There has been some increase in the use of beer and wine, but the total absolute alcohol volume has declined. This probably indicates that some regular drinkers have become occasional drinkers and that the number of abstainers has increased.

We do not know the reasons for the decline in use of alcohol. The decline is as yet rather small.

ALCOHOL IN LITERATURE

The average citizen of these days has ample opportunity to hear that alcohol is a problem. *The Lost Weekend,* by Charles Jackson, awakened many people to the problem of the alcoholic. The movie version of the story stimulated sale of the book. Real sympathy for the alcoholic as a victim was stirred up.

Drinking problems have loomed large in several of the plays of Tennessee Williams. *Cat on a Hot Tin Roof* dealt sympathetically and realistically with the problems of alcoholism. Eugene O'Neill's *A Touch of the Poet* is another play that deals realistically with alcohol as a complicating factor in human problems.

Many motion pictures still glorify the use of alcohol. Serious literature, however, makes no such mistake. Dylan Thomas and his alcoholic death linger too fresh in the memory for light, sophisticated treatment of alcohol to have any place in serious works.

EDUCATION AND PROPAGANDA

All the states require education about alcohol as a part of the public school curriculum. The opportunities for dealing with this difficult problem area are substantial. Many schools do not know how education about alcohol may be undertaken since the subject is controversial. Texts have given only a few pages to alcohol as a physiological problem.

Yale University is now in its second decade of assisting the public schools to deal with alcohol education. It has conducted surveys, suggested curricula, assisted in the preparation of texts and teaching aids, and conducted summer schools with special work for public school teachers and administrators.[10]

While these forces are at work, seeking to inform the public about alcohol problems, other forces are at work seeking to manipulate the public into acceptance of alcohol. Nowhere are the "hidden persuaders" more at work than in the field of alcohol advertising. Manufacturers and sellers of alcoholic products regularly spend large amounts of money through the various media of advertising. Newspapers, magazines, radio, television, and billboard displays are all heavily patronized by the alcohol industry. So much money has been spent that the impression is frequently left that the media could not continue in business without the continued advertising of alcohol.

There are some radio and television stations and many newspapers and magazines that refuse to accept advertising from the alcohol industry.

The economic power of the advertising dollar is a powerful censor on the staff of some news media. Stories favoring alcohol are given prominent attention. Stories about the twenty-fifth anniversary of repeal were printed as news stories. These propaganda handouts twisted facts and presented material which

---

[10] McCarthy and Douglas, *op. cit.*, Part II, pp. 141-278.

could not have been called news by any stretch of the imagination.[11]

Every political campaign which seeks to initiate new controls on the sale or use of alcohol is the occasion for more tension in our society. Newspapers carry reports of violent statements by both sides. The ghost of prohibition is revived, and the public is assured that the gangsters are just around the corner, ready to take control of the nation.

Little opportunity is given for any sane discussion by legislators of an adequate program of social control. Lobbyists immediately rush in to present partisan pictures before any objective, impartial study can be undertaken.

When in local-option elections the electorate votes against the sale of alcohol, alcohol interests often refuse to accept the results of the election. Injunctions are sought to prevent the execution of the measure passed in the election. New elections are immediately sought. All these legal moves are carried on in an atmosphere of hostility which further separates citizens who hold different views concerning the proper control of alcohol.

AGREEMENT AMONG THE CHURCHES

The confusion is made worse by differences between churches as they speak on the issues arising from the use of alcohol. The churches differ peaceably on many issues, but the alcohol question has aroused unchristian attitudes and spurred contentious actions. When the churches fight each other—whatever the issue—they add to the confusion of society.

The confusion between the churches is largely unnecessary. The major religions of this nation—Protestant, Catholic, Jew— are all agreed that drunkenness is sin. In a nation so filled with the sin of drunkenness as ours, the religions have a common message concerning the misuse of alcohol upon which they could agree. Each religious group has in its midst respected

---

[11] See Associated Press story by Tom Henshaw for release on December 1, 1958.

religionists who practice abstinence from the use of alcohol. With these points of common concern, conversations should be undertaken to discover other areas of agreement.

Not all differences between religious groups or within our society are going to be erased. Some will continue to hold that alcohol is God's creation, made for man's use and enjoyment. Moderate drinking will continue to be esteemed by some churchmen as within the will of God. Others will continue to regard any use of alcoholic beverages as contrary to the will of God. All good citizens and all good Christians can agree that clearly established misuse of alcohol which endangers society and innocent persons must be stopped. Good citizens and good Christians of different persuasions can work together and devise strategies for immediate solutions to the grossest forms of misuse of alcohol.

CHAPTER II

The Need for Control

THERE is no argument but that alcohol is frequently mis-used in our society. The various branches of the alcohol industry admit as much. Through the industries they seek to police some of the retailers who are responsible for some of the grossest crimes.

The alcohol industry is subject to continuous supervision and control by the various levels of government. The alcohol indus-try is a licensed business. This does not emphasize that distill-eries and breweries are legal businesses. Rather it emphasizes that they are businesses engaging in practices which are poten-tially harmful to society. These business concerns are licensed so that the government may exercise strict control over the production and distribution of all alcohol.

The potential harm present in all branches of the alcohol industry can be clearly shown by the regulatory provisions of the various governmental agencies. In most localities any re-tailer of alcohol is required to be a person of good character and without previous record of difficulties with law enforcement agencies. Various governmental units regulate the location of retail liquor stores, prohibiting nearness to schools and churches. Closing hours are generally imposed. Unaccompanied women are sometimes excluded from bars. Retail liquor stores are generally required to close during voting hours on election days. Minors are forbidden to buy drinks and frequently are excluded from the premises of retail liquor stores. All these regulations are unusual rules for business establishments. They clearly indicate the dangerous character of the liquor industry and its need for social control.

Various agencies cooperate to warn that drinking and driving constitute a serious misuse of alcohol. Among the groups concerned about the drinking driver is the liquor industry. The alcohol manufacturers steadily warn against drinking and driving.

LEGAL CONTROL

In some states retailers of liquor are legally responsible for the actions of any persons to whom liquor is sold while the purchaser is intoxicated. In others retailers are liable for the intoxicated behavior of minors to whom alcohol is sold. These laws recognize in principle that intoxicated persons are apt to engage in irresponsible or anti-social activities.

Statistics concerning intoxication are inadequate. Only records of public drunkenness, usually associated with some form of misdemeanor or felony, are generally available. Intoxication is far more frequent than the booking of inebriates in police court. Yet alcohol-related arrests account for at least 45 per cent of all arrests made. In 1958 there were 2,340,000 arrests for various crimes in cities of 2,500 and over. Alleged drunkenness accounted for 909,000 of these, while disorderly conduct accounted for 282,000 more.[1]

PREVALENCE OF ALCOHOL

Despite the problems arising from the use of alcohol, it is still widely used as a beverage. The alcoholic beverage industry has a very substantial interest in continuing the use of alcohol. Alcoholic beverage outlets outnumber all churches in the nation by more than 131,000. In 1957 there were 438,000 retail dealers selling alcoholic beverages.[2]

The consumption of alcoholic beverages is not uniform throughout the nation. Rural areas have lower per capita con-

---

[1] *Uniform Crime Reports for the United States: 1958,* Washington: Government Printing Office, 1959, p. 93.

[2] *Statistics Relating to the Alcohol and Tobacco Industries,* Internal Revenue Service, June 30, 1957, Table I.
Benson Y. Landis, *1959 Yearbook of American Churches,* National Council of Churches of Christ in the USA, New York, 1958, p. 267.

sumption of alcohol than do urban areas. Metropolitan areas have the highest rate of consumption of alcohol of any type of community. Drinking is more common in areas having the higher percentages of foreign-born. The areas of greatest strength for the Protestant churches are also the areas of lowest consumption of alcohol. The outstanding exception to these trends is the state of Nevada. Nevada leads the nation in per capita consumption of alcohol and in the rate of alcoholism.

The number of persons who drink is very difficult to determine. Persons hesitate to indicate to a poll-taker their drinking patterns. The Gallup public opinion poll shows wide variations in its reports concerning the use of alcoholic beverages. The Gallup poll of May, 1960, reports that approximately 64,900,000 Americans use some form of alcoholic beverage. From this figure we are informed that 62 per cent of the adults in the nation use alcoholic beverages. In 1945 a similar poll had indicated that 67 per cent of the adult population used intoxicants.

Various other studies of samples of population support the estimate that from 60 to 65 per cent of the adult population use alcoholic beverages. These studies are often referred to in popular journals and news media. These other studies, however, are from seven to ten years old. The figures probably are accurate for the period of 1950, but evidently there are significant changes occurring in drinking patterns.

Large amounts of money continue to be spent for alcoholic beverages. Approximately eleven to twelve billion dollars per year are spent for alcohol for which the Federal tax has been paid. Taxes on alcoholic beverages are constantly being raised. With new revenues needed by all governmental units, new taxes are necessary. The liquor trade is one that finds little support relative to taxation. The taxes raise the price of liquor and make bootlegging more profitable. The unlawful manufacture and sale of alcoholic beverages continues to pose one of the most prevalent of law enforcement problems in the United States.

BOOTLEGGING

Bootlegging is a big business in this nation. Bootlegging may involve the sale of alcoholic beverages legally manufactured and taxed, but illegally sold in areas forbidding the sale of alcoholic beverages. It may involve the sale of alcoholic beverages legally manufactured and taxed, but upon which proper state or local taxes have not been paid. It also may involve the sale of alcohol illegally manufactured and upon which no tax has been paid.

Agents of the Treasury Department of the Federal government are constantly seeking illegal liquor stills. These are discovered in operation in suburban neighborhoods or downtown warehouses of metropolitan areas as well as in the mountains of the southern Appalachians. More illegal stills of larger capacity are now being discovered than during any previous period. These stills are uncovered in areas where legal sales of alcohol are allowed as well as in areas in which alcoholic beverages are not legally sold.

The alcohol industry, the governments, and the churches are all opposed to this widespread illegal sale of alcohol by bootleggers, but for different reasons. The bootlegger is unfair competition to the distillers. The bootlegger is a tax evader and violator of pure food regulations to the governments. The churches oppose the bootlegger because of the complete lack of social control of this menace. The churches recognize that bootleggers corrupt law enforcement officials today just as they did thirty years ago. No bootlegger can stay in business long unless there is failure on the part of some law enforcement officer to do his duty.

Minors are forbidden by law from buying liquor. The states also forbid the sale of beer or wine to youth. If the youth wish to drink, they may seek out bootleggers. Usually they find means, however, for obtaining alcohol from legal outlets. One of the group of youth may be old enough to purchase alcohol legally. At any rate, young people are able to obtain alcohol in many localities.

28

WHO DOES THE DRINKING?

The incidence of drinking among high school youth varies widely from region to region. A study of Kansas youth indicated that drinking by high school students was relatively infrequent. Other studies of metropolitan areas indicate frequent use of alcohol by high school students. In one study only 12 per cent of the students did not use alcoholic beverages.[3]

Many young adults drink some form of alcoholic beverage. The studies of drinking in college indicate that about 75 per cent of the students use alcohol. In all studies the percentage of adults who drink declines with increase in age. It is likely, therefore, that young adults in the early twenties are more apt to drink than any other age segment of our population. It is also likely that many who drink at this age stop drinking as they grow older.

More men than women drink. The incidence of drinking among women is increasing. The incidence of alcoholism among women is also increasing. It is possible that women are now drinking more openly than formerly when taboos were firmly established against women drinking. It is also possible that a number of women are now drinking to keep their husbands company. One advertising company found that most of the beer purchasers in the United States were women. The client of this advertising agency redesigned its beer bottle to appeal to the aesthetic sensibilities of the women.[4]

Drinkers can be classified according to the frequency with which they drink and the amount and type of alcohol consumed. These classifications are chiefly valuable for descriptive purposes. Individuals rarely report properly as to the amount of alcoholic beverages consumed or as to the frequency with which drinking occurs. For many people drinking is so charged with emotional reactions that memories of drinking tend to be

---

[3] McCarthy, *op. cit.*, pp. 205-218.

[4] Vance Parkard, *The Hidden Persuaders,* New York: David McKay Company, Inc., 1957, pp. 94-95. Also note Martin Mayer, *Madison Avenue, U.S.A.,* New York: Harper & Brothers, 1958, p. 214.

colored. Drinking may affect the memory so that quantities drunk may be misrepresented due to faulty recollection. Statistical studies of drinkers by classification are, therefore, highly suspect.

The occasional drinker uses alcohol infrequently. Alcohol is just one part of the celebration of a very "special occasion." These special occasions may diminish with age so that many so-called occasional drinkers may actually be very near abstinence. The person may still classify himself as an occasional drinker because he does not wish to be classified as an abstainer.

The moderate regular drinker does not place any limitations on the frequency of his drinking. He drinks when the social occasions seem to call for drinking behavior. He usually does not drink to the point of noticeable intoxication, but his frequent drinking situations make him a practiced drinker with abilities to hide the effects of mild intoxication.

The heavy drinker is the drinker who usually drinks to excess. The frequency of his drinking may not be as great as that of the moderate regular drinker. The heavy drinker obviously drinks for the effect of intoxication.[5] He may drink to escape harsh reality, or he may drink from long habit. The heavy drinker may be able to continue his drinking bouts without becoming an alcoholic. Many heavy drinkers, however, are alcoholics who have not yet slid to the bottom. The chronic drunk of the police court may fit in this category, or he may be an alcoholic.

The alcoholic is a compulsive drinker. He cannot drink without becoming intoxicated. He has deep personality disturbances which he seeks to escape by drinking. His drinking in turn creates new problems for him. The alcoholic is unable to control his drinking or to stop drinking without help. There are more than five million alcoholics in this nation.

Occasional drinkers and regular moderate drinkers do not believe that they constitute any problem for society. The prob-

[5] Vance Parkard, *The Hidden Persuaders*, p. 41.

lems arising from heavy drinkers and alcoholics are easily seen. Few heavy drinkers or alcoholics began drinking with any intent to be other than moderate drinkers. Many moderate drinkers lose control of their drinking patterns, although numerous moderate drinkers remain in complete control of their drinking habits.

Moderate drinkers often underestimate the degree to which they are affected by alcohol or are "under the influence." A situation which seems completely controlled to the moderate drinker may be regarded differently by the objective observer. The moderate drinker is not the most trustworthy judge of the effects of his own actions. These untrustworthy judgments are amply demonstrated by the drinking driver.

It is very difficult to weigh the importance of the use of alcoholic beverages as related to certain social problems. Some observers cite the importance of alcohol as a contributing factor in the causation of a problem. Other observers see any relationship to alcohol as incidental rather than the cause. The very complexity of many social problems makes it impossible to settle which factors are causative and which are casually related. Great caution must be exercised against accepting any analysis of a major social problem, or solution to it, unless the evidence presented is clear-cut and conclusive.

ALCOHOL AND JUVENILE DELINQUENCY

One very complex problem in our society is the high rate of juvenile delinquency. Numerous theories have been advanced for the cause or causes of juvenile delinquency. Other theories are advanced to account for the very significant increase in juvenile delinquency. Some of the theories contradict other theories. Yet, many of these theories seem to be rational conclusions drawn from research.

It is impossible to determine the full importance of alcohol as a contributing factor in the increase of juvenile delinquency. It is, without question, a vital consideration. Obviously it contrib-

31

utes to the high incidence of juvenile delinquency since juvenile use of alcohol is an offense against the law. A juvenile can be declared delinquent because he has used alcohol. In some states the law prohibits juveniles from drinking even though the drinking occurs at home and in the presence of the parents.

Alcohol-related offenses do not account for juvenile offenses to the same degree as for adult offenses. Public drunkenness and breach of peace presumably are more common among adults than among juveniles.

In the troubles with juveniles in New York City alcohol is mentioned as a factor. In an interview with gang members one leader talked to a Youth Board worker:

"I like to rumble (gang fight) sometimes. It makes me feel good. When I get high, like drinking, I like it. Sure a guy can get shot up. Do I know what I'm doing? Sure. I don't get too high." [6]

Commissioner Ralph W. Whelan of the New York City Youth Board reported on the fact that less than 1 per cent of the city's families produced more than 75 per cent of the juvenile delinquency:

"These families are beset by a host of serious problems, including alcoholism, drug addiction, mental illness, desertion, and youth crime." [7]

Much of juvenile delinquency can best be understood as rebellious acts against adult authority, particularly parental authority. Drinking of alcohol by juveniles may well begin as rebellious behavior. Drinking may be a part of a larger complex of rebellious behavior. Under such circumstances the use of alcohol is a symptom of the basic problem of rebellion against authority. This use of alcohol need not be considered the cause of juvenile delinquency, but any continued use will probably contribute to other forms of delinquent behavior.

---

[6] Gertrude Samuels, "Why 'The Assassins' Can't Be Punks," *The New York Times Magazine*, August 16, 1959, p. 84.

[7] News release of August 30, 1959.

The use of alcohol by youth weakens inhibitions at the very time when they are already subject to the heaviest attack. Sexual mores and injunctions against fast and reckless driving are violated by many youth who do not use alcohol. The use of alcohol does weaken the ability of the judgment to accept the mores and injunctions of society.

Social workers in homes for unwed mothers have stated that the use of alcohol by young girls is an important factor contributing to the illegitimate pregnancy. Some workers indicate that the use of alcohol as a contributing factor to juvenile sexual delinquency is steadily increasing in importance.

It is unlikely that alcohol is the major causative factor in very much juvenile delinquency. It is highly probable, however, that the use of alcohol is a contributing factor in a large percentage of the cases of juvenile delinquency.

ALCOHOL AND MARITAL TROUBLES

The problems arising from family disorganization are also complex and difficult of analysis. Marital discord, as evidenced by marriages broken through divorce or separation, has become a matter of increasing concern. The number of divorces is substantially greater than at any time prior to World War II. Many attempts have been made to explain the rise in family disorganization by reference to factors which have changed since World War II.

The rise in marital discord as indicated by statistics of broken marriages cannot be easily explained by reference to any set of external factors. Cultural changes and the interplay of psychodynamic forces are of major importance in interpreting the rise in broken marriages, but these forces cannot be reduced to simple statistical tables and formulae.

Certain external factors are quite important in any study of marital discord, even when the importance of the personal psychodynamic forces is accepted as primary. One such external factor which contributes to many cases of marital discord is the use of alcohol. The use of alcohol may be of little importance in many families, but in others it may loom large as a major source of tension underlying marital discord.

Habitual drunkenness is recognized in a number of the states as sufficient grounds for divorce action. Many divorces granted for reasons of cruelty involve excessive use of alcohol. Divorces granted because of desertion and non-support often involve excessive drinking also. The alleged grounds for divorce are insufficient explanation of the many factors operative in the marital discord which lead to dissolution of the marriage.

Studies of alcoholism indicate that virtually all families of alcoholics are torn by marital discord. Most men married to alcoholic wives get divorces rather quickly. The wives of alcoholic husbands frequently threaten divorce, although few do secure them, despite the hectic disturbances.

Any pastor or marriage counselor can witness to the frequency with which he encounters marital problems involving the use of alcohol. A change in drinking patterns for many families must occur before more satisfactory marital adjustments can be obtained.

THE DRINKING DRIVER

One of the important social problems of our nation is the great loss of life and property due to automobile accidents. The auto accident problem is not so complex as the problems of juvenile delinquency and marital discord. The importance of alcoholic beverages as causative factors in accidents is more easily established. Here too, however, the statistics are not thoroughly adequate; alcohol is involved in far more accidents than reports indicate. Due to the penalties invoked against drinking drivers, officers often ignore the use of alcohol and record some other violation. Drinking drivers are often charged with reckless driving or negligent collision rather than with driving under the influence of alcohol. The National Safety Council and other agencies concerned with traffic safety have sought better reporting of the use of alcohol by drivers involved in accidents.

Legal difficulties hamper accurate assessment of the extent of drunken driving. At least forty-six states have laws recognizing chemical tests of the alcoholic content of the blood as adequate basis for conviction of driving under the influence of alcohol. In numerous situations, however, the driver must consent to the chemical testing. Clinical observation of the motor skills of a driver suspected of drinking is not nearly so adequate as are various chemical tests. These legal safeguards of the individual's right to privacy definitely work against the detection, conviction, or reporting of the drinking driver.

The Uniform Vehicle Code establishes a concentration of 0.15 per cent alcohol in the blood as proof of intoxication. This feature of the Uniform Vehicle Code represents a great advance over previous laws. Research indicates, however, that the law can be improved.

As a result of their research Drs. Loomis and West observe: "Pharmacologically, alcohol would indeed be a peculiar drug if it produced no significant effect at a blood concentration of 0.14 per cent but a significant effect at 0.15 per cent. Yet this is essentially the stand taken by the legal profession with the establishment of such laws." [8]

These investigators conclude: "The results of the present study indicate that blood alcohol levels well below 0.15 per cent induce measurable objective impairment of the functions tested in the simulated driving test. All the subjects showed some impairment of function at blood alcohol concentrations of 0.05 per cent. Current law is thus too lenient, since impairment of function is present before the legal limit of blood alcohol concentration is reached. If the intention of such a law is to enable legal action to be taken when impairment of function is present, then 0.05 per cent alcohol in the blood should be considered as the

---

[8] "The Influence of Alcohol on Automobile Driving Ability," *Quarterly Journal of Studies on Alcohol*, Vol. XIX, No. 1, March 1958, p. 31.

base level at which a person is under the influence of alcohol for the purpose of driving an automobile." [9]

If the recommendations of these experts were to be heeded, the reports of the effects of alcohol on driving would be greatly increased. Even with the present standards the problem is acute. The full picture that would be presented by accurate data of the number of drinking drivers involved in accidents would be even more frightening.

More than 40,000 persons are killed each year in automobile accidents. The most recent data from the National Safety Council indicate that a drinking driver was involved in at least 30 per cent of the fatal accidents of 1956. Drinking, then, is an important causative factor in at least 12,000 traffic deaths *annually*.

Drinking at holiday seasons increases the proportion of alcohol-induced accidental deaths. The Christmas season is marred by about 700 traffic fatalities, of which 55 per cent are caused by drinking drivers. Nearly 400 deaths each Christmas holiday stem from the drinking driver!

Many drinking drivers continue to operate vehicles, endan-

[9] *Ibid.*, p. 44.

PERCENTAGE OF FATAL ACCIDENTS IN WHICH DRINKERS ARE INVOLVED

1948   17%

1956   30%

Data from National Safety Council
One Symbol Equals 5%

gering lives, even after their licenses are suspended or revoked. A resident of Louisville, Kentucky, wrote to the newspaper after it reported that 9,600 drinking Kentuckians had just lost their driver's licenses. He suggested that the state remove the license plates from the automobile of the drinking driver who had lost his driver's license. He hoped by some such plan to get the drinking driver off the road. He concluded: "I am not opposed to drinking, but I say it is time for Kentuckians to rise up and demand strict law enforcement to cover this needless damage and slaughter." [10] All citizens, whether they use alcohol or not, should unite to force drinking drivers to stop their driving.

Social drinkers frequently drive home from parties at which they have consumed alcohol. Many of these do not regard themselves as drinking drivers; they feel that they are not under the influence of alcohol. The National Safety Council warns these persons that "small amounts of alcohol reduce self-control and driving ability. . . . It takes at least three hours to oxidize one ounce of pure alcohol. Two cocktails may reduce visual acuity as much as wearing dark sun glasses at night. . . . Coffee or other stimulants will not offset the effects of alcohol. Only *time* can eliminate alcohol from the blood stream." [11]

The proportion of drinking drivers involved in fatal accidents is steadily increasing. Drinking drivers were involved in 17 per cent of the fatal accidents in 1948, but by 1956 the percentage had climbed to 30. All our traffic education and superhighways will be of little value if the drinking driver problem continues to worsen. McCarthy and Douglass have commented on the problem of the drinking driver: "It is as immoral to kill or maim through negligence with an automobile as through negligence with a rifle. Beyond the ethical question, the problem is one of concern to police and motor vehicle departments; it becomes a responsibility of the seller and buyer of liquor; and

---

[10] Quoted in Louisville *Courier-Journal,* August 14, 1959.
[11] *Fact Sheet,* National Safety Council, Chicago.

37

it is the cause of immeasurable loss to the victim's family. Driving a car after drinking, or riding with an operator who has been drinking, is viewed too lightly by too many persons." [12]

ECONOMIC COSTS

The toll of lives attributable to the drinking driver arouses our sympathies. The economic losses arising from the drinking driver are very great. Many of these losses are difficult to estimate. Many of the costs are borne by persons who do not drink or are in no way responsible for the accidents. Automobile insurance rates are determined after consideration of the previous year's accident loss figures. All of us help pay for the costs of the accidents of the past year.

In many spheres of economics alcohol is a wastrel. The economic costs of alcohol are gigantic. All statistical studies of the economic costs of alcohol indicate their incompleteness. Many of the economic wastes attributable to the use of alcohol cannot be adequately determined. The various studies do indicate that the costs to be charged against alcohol run into the *billions*.

The law enforcement costs related to the use of alcohol must be substantial in view of the reports from the F. B. I. that more than 1,500,000 persons are arrested each year on charges of drunkenness, drunken driving, and other alcohol-related offenses. The fines and other revenues derived from these offenders fall far short of paying the costs of apprehension, trial, and punishment.

Alcohol taxes do pay into the various governments substantial amounts. Taxes to all governmental levels paid by alcohol interests will total approximately five billion dollars. This revenue is not, however, net gain for the governments. The tax paid to the federal government is substantial revenue; and since that government does not provide services for alcohol-related offenses to the degree that the states do, a substantial

---

[12] McCarthy and Douglass, *op. cit.*, pp. 125-6.

net gain is made by the federal government. During 1959 the national government appropriated $750,000 for research on alcoholism. The federal government could well afford to make this an annual appropriation as long as needed in view of the revenues it derives from alcohol. Annually the federal government receives more than four thousand times as much revenue from alcohol taxes as its expenditure on research on alcoholism. The annual receipts of the federal government from alcohol taxes exceed $3,000,000,000.

The picture with the state governments is entirely different. The states are required to furnish many more services related to alcohol-caused expenses. Several studies have indicated that state governments run net losses in connection with revenues and expenditures from alcohol. The states spend from $1.50 to $7.50 in *direct* alcohol-caused expenses for every $1.00 collected as taxes levied upon alcohol.

In 1943 the General Court of Massachusetts established a special commission to investigate the problem of drunkenness. The report indicated that in 1943 the alcohol tax revenue for the state, cities, and towns of the state was $13,139,000. In the same year, *known* alcohol-related losses to the state in terms of penal costs, rehabilitation expenses, and welfare funds was $46,475,000. The commission stated that the losses listed were minimal figures and that completely comprehensive figures would probably run 10 per cent higher. This study revealed that Massachusetts spent at least $3.50 because of alcohol for every $1.00 collected in taxes on beer, wine, and liquor.

A study in Utah in 1956 reported that the state has spent more than $6,000,000 annually for jailing alcoholics, providing medical attention for them, fighting crime resulting from alcoholism, and making up lost time and wages in industry. During 1955 the state of Utah had collected $4,163,000 from taxes on alcoholic beverages and license fees for sale of alcoholic beverages. Although the expenses included only the costs arising from *alcoholism*—not all drinking—it is apparent that the state suffers a net loss from the alcoholic trade. For every $1.00 collected from alcohol taxes, it spends $1.50 on costs of alcoholism.

A similar study from California in 1955 indicated revenues from alcohol of $39,000,000. The annual cost of alcoholism in the state for the same period was estimated as at least $120,000,-000, but possibly as much as $300,000,000.

If the figures from these three states are indicative of the entire nation—and there is every reason to believe that they are —the total costs of alcohol substantially exceed the revenues derived from alcohol. The states suffer a net loss from the alcohol trade. It is also to be remembered that the alcohol industry only collects the taxes from the purchaser. The consumer of alcohol pays the tax.

ALCOHOL TAX REVENUE AND ALCOHOL COSTS*
IN CERTAIN STATES

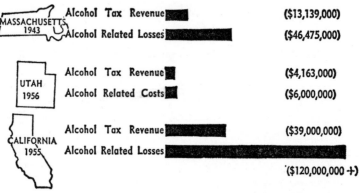

MASSACHUSETTS 1943
Alcohol Tax Revenue ($13,139,000)
Alcohol Related Losses ($46,475,000)

UTAH 1956
Alcohol Tax Revenue ($4,163,000)
Alcohol Related Costs ($6,000,000)

CALIFORNIA 1955
Alcohol Tax Revenue ($39,000,000)
Alcohol Related Losses ($120,000,000 +)

¼"=10 Million

* These are known alcohol related losses to the state in terms of rehabilitation, welfare, etc.

COSTS TO INDUSTRY

No adequate study has ever been made of the costs to industry arising from the use of alcohol. The National Safety Council recognizes the use of alcohol as a factor contributing to industrial accidents. Any study of industrial losses attributable to alcohol must include losses from absenteeism and inefficiency due to drinking.

Rather reliable data have been gathered to report the costs of alcoholism. The National Industrial Conference Board estimates that there are 2,000,000 alcoholics in industry, or about three per cent of the labor force. Among alcoholics absenteeism is much more common than among other workers. Male alcoholics have an absenteeism rate three times as high as the average, while female alcoholics have an absenteeism rate twice as high as average.

Alcoholics often report to work while suffering from a hangover. The worker suffering from a hangover is described by Dr. Milton A. Maxwell as "a half man." The alcoholic suffering from a hangover is frequently able to conceal his inefficiency by practices which he has devised over a long period of drinking. It is impossible to set a value upon the great loss of productive capacity resulting from the hangover. Dr. Maxwell also points out that many important administrative decisions are made by management personnel suffering from hangovers. The loss from bad administrative decisions endangers the financial well-being of the entire company, affecting the economic welfare of nondrinkers as well as drinkers.

It is impossible to determine—even approximately—the economic costs of alcoholic drink. A study reported in *Fortune* magazine indicates the costs as substantial. It tells of instances in which alcoholic executives made poor decisions costing hundreds of thousands, even millions of dollars.[12]

---

[12] "The Alcoholic Executive," January, 1960.

ALCOHOL AND CRIME

The alcohol business confronts society with another problem in its relations to crime. The alcohol industry constantly tells the public that Prohibition was responsible for the gangsters in this nation. There is no denying that the gangster element did supply bootleg whiskey to nearly anyone who wished to purchase it. Various hoodlum gangs did receive billions of dollars from the illicit liquor traffic. The Prohibition era did not, however, create the gangsters. Neither was bootleg whiskey the sole source of income of these gangs during the Prohibition era. Al Capone got his start as a gangster on the southside of Chicago running a brothel in the pre-Prohibition era. His gang had major receipts from prostitution, narcotics, and gambling.

The gangster element in our nation was not eliminated with the coming of Repeal. It is well known that these gangsters continue to ply their vicious rackets in our day. The Kefauver Committee, the McClellan Committee, and various other investigating agencies have revealed to us the close ties between some gangsters and the legal alcohol business.

It is perhaps unfair to place all blame on the alcohol business for allowing these gangsters to get into the trade. Stocks of breweries have been bought on the stock exchange; there are no laws to prohibit such purchases. These gangster elements have also engaged in irregular and questionable practices, however.

The McClellan Committee has recently disclosed that Chicago hoodlums Gus Alex and Tony Accardo have received thousands of dollars for "salesmanship" in forcing cafe and tavern owners to buy beer from their employers. Recently in Chicago retail licenses have been granted to disreputable associates of long-time gangsters. Investigations indicate that other license holders serve as "fronts" for gangsters who control taverns and bars.

The alcohol industry should stop talking about the gangster element in the Prohibition era and work instead on cleaning out the disreputable element in the industry today. Other trades and professions are able to police themselves. If the alcohol industry needs help in terms of new laws and protective regulations against the lawless element, such help could be sought from the legislatures by the well-paid lobbyists already on the staff of the industry.

AN INTERNATIONAL PROBLEM

In many parts of the world the drinking patterns of the United States are beyond comprehension. Nationals of other countries most frequently draw their opinions of this nation from partial and fragmentary information. Many "ugly Americans" traveling abroad or working overseas hurt the reputation of their homeland by their drinking patterns. Numerous Hollywood pictures of Americans present wholesale drinking as an integral part of American life.

The use of alcohol is a problem of importance in some phases of international relations. A little alcohol loosens the tongue. Secret information can be blurted out in an unguarded moment —and alcohol removes one guard from monitoring the tongue. Richard J. Healy, security chief for a Los Angeles electronics research and development firm, said that loose tongues rather than deliberate traitors or planted Russian agents are the biggest threat to America's security.[13] Mr. Healy is national president of the American Society of Industrial Security.

The cocktail party is a commonplace feature of our nation's diplomacy. Tongues can be loose in cocktail parties just as surely as in bars. Newspapers and magazines have published classified material related at cocktail parties by drinking Congressmen. Military leaders may have some justification for hesitancy to tell certain Congressmen of military plans.

Indian embassies throughout the world do not serve liquor at their parties. Prime Minister Nehru observed, "If people are attracted only by our drinks, they had better stay away." He

---

[13] In a speech delivered in Dallas, Texas, on January 16, 1959, to the North Texas Chapter of the American Society of Industrial Security. Reported in Dallas *Morning News*, January 17, 1959.

added, "You know, some officials tend to get loose-tongued under the influence of drinks and leak secrets."

Apart from the danger of loose tongues, the cocktail parties are expensive luxuries which this nation can ill afford at any time. As we strive for a balanced budget for the national government, it seems wasteful to spend a million dollars for whiskey for governmental cocktail parties. Yet, the State Department requested an even million dollars for "whiskey money" in the fiscal year 1958-1959.

The State Department can entertain without alcohol. A party held in Washington in late 1957 in honor of Mohammed V, King of Morocco, served orange juice, tomato juice, and fruit punch, but no alcoholic beverages. It would seem advisable for officials in the State Department to consider the additional item of information that orange juice is the favorite drink in the United Nations bar in the U. N. headquarters in New York.

The use of alcohol can easily offend nationals of many other countries. Moslem nations rigidly forbid the use of alcohol. Citizens of this nation working in the oil fields of Saudi Arabia have offended King Ibn Saud by their violation of his decrees against all intoxicants.[14] It is a sorry picture when citizens of this nation that believes in freedom of religion assail the leader of another nation because of his religious convictions against the use of alcohol. It is indeed a disturbing thought that a Moslem nation should stand for abstinence, while it is the representatives of a Christian nation that demand the right to get drunk.

[14] *Time*, December 22, 1952, p. 30.

Chapter III

Alcoholism—a Modern Disease

WITHIN the past ten to fifteen years many American citizens have come to recognize alcoholism as a modern disease. Attitudes associated with illness have begun to replace. the disgust and disdain formerly felt toward the alcoholic. What has caused these changes of attitude? Is the alcoholic really sick?

It has been known for some time that the alcoholic is a major factor in producing the social problems arising from the use of intoxicants. The alcoholic is a problem for the law enforcement officers of every city. The economic costs of alcoholism represent a major proportion of the economic waste arising from the use of alcoholic beverages. Alcoholics have notable difficulties in marriage adjustments. They are frequently involved in automobile accidents. Alcoholism is a major contributing factor to several social problems.

Alcoholism has become so prevalent throughout the nation as a disruptive factor in social relations that it merits classification as a social problem. It is also classified as a health problem. Still other classifications are possible.

FIVE MILLION ALCOHOLICS

Alcoholism is so prevalent today that contact with alcoholics is almost universal. Most clergymen have become well acquainted with alcoholics through the requests of relatives for help. Alcoholics are members of numerous churches, but many still shun the churches. Within our society nearly every person has some relative or friend who is an alcoholic.

Not all alcoholics recognize their condition. Many are unwilling to be classified as alcoholic. In other situations relatives are far more resistant to any such classification. For many persons in our society the term alcoholic is still a stigma of disgrace. No significant recovery can occur until the alcoholic condition is recognized. Any disgrace or shame associated with alcoholism makes self-recognition and therapy more difficult.

The alcoholic has been the subject of many moralistic lectures. His condition has been described as stemming from sinfulness and an unwillingness to cease drinking. Alcoholism is a moral problem, but moralistic lectures are of little benefit to the alcoholic. He is no longer able by exercise of will to stop drinking. He must be assisted by others as well as by God if he is to stop.

The alcoholic cannot drink moderately. He cannot be sure at any time when he will stop drinking. One small drink sets into motion a cycle of events beyond his control. The alcoholic can become sober, but he never ceases to be an alcoholic. The reformed alcoholic is more accurately referred to as a sober alcoholic; no reformation process can transform the alcoholic into a person who can use alcohol in small amounts.

There is no universally accepted standard definition of alcoholism. Many discussions of the problem proceed without definition. All of these discussions refer to the condition in which the drinker has major problems arising from his inability to use alcohol as a beverage of moderation.

The best statistics on the prevalence of alcoholism have been collected for the Yale University Center of Alcohol Studies by Mark Keller and Vera Efron. The definition used by them was developed by E. M. Jellinek and Mark Keller: "Alcoholics are those excessive drinkers whose dependence upon alcohol has attained such a degree that it shows a noticeable mental disturbance, or an interference with their bodily or mental health, their interpersonal relations, and their smooth social and economic functioning; or who show prodromal * signs of such developments."

The prodromal phase of the alcoholic is the preliminary phase in which intoxication is not severe and is usually limited to evenings or occasional week-ends. The drinking is not conspicuous in this phase. Very rarely does a drinker in the prodromal phase appear to the public to be an alcoholic. Yet, even at this early stage, the alcoholic is rapidly losing control over his drinking patterns. Since the criterion of alcoholism is the loss of control over the alcoholic intake, the alcoholic who has reached only the preliminary prodromal phase is sometimes regarded already as an alcoholic.

Statistics on alcoholics are reported in two categories by Keller and Efron. Alcoholics are classified by reference to problems stemming from drinking: alcoholics with complications and alcoholics without complications. Alcoholics with complications are those who have developed recognizable physical or mental symptoms due to excessive drinking. The alcoholics without complications have developed social patterns which indicate that their drinking constitutes a problem.

THE PROBLEM DRINKER

Frequently reference is made to the problem drinker. The class of the problem drinker includes both alcoholics and drinkers in the prodromal or pre-alcoholic stage. The problem drinker is defined as a person whose excessive drinking repeatedly interferes with his health or personal relations, and whose work is thereby reduced in efficiency and dependability.

Alcoholics usually have a history of moderate drinking preceding any appearance of problem drinking. The alcoholic usually passes through a regular sequence in his change from moderate drinking to uncontrolled drinking. A knowledge of the steps

---

* "Prod'ro-mal" is the medical term used to describe the early stages or warning symptoms of a disease. Literally, from the Greek words *pro* (before) and *dromos* (running), a prodrome is a "running before"; it is defined as a premonitory symptom. The prodromal phase of a disease is the stage at which warning symptoms appear.

leading to alcoholism can assist in the early detection and re-habilitation of alcoholic drinkers.

The social drinker enters the prodromal phase leading to alcoholism when he suffers his first blackout. In the blackout there is a partial amnesia without loss of consciousness. The blackout may occur even during drinking in which no intoxication seems present. If blackouts begin to occur frequently after the consumption of moderate amounts of alcohol, future alcohol addiction is indicated if drinking continues. If blackouts occur in 30 per cent of the drinking bouts, danger is clearly present.

The problem drinker in the pre-alcoholic phase is unable to drink in the same pattern as formerly. He sneaks drinks when others are not looking. He may gulp his drinks to hasten the effect of drinking—and to make possible more drinking. He begins to worry about the adequacy of the supply of liquor at social occasions. Drink becomes a necessity, but he avoids speaking about it to others from fear that they will notice how different are his drinking patterns. Alcohol, classified medically as an anesthetic, has become for him a drug.

Many excessive drinkers continue to drink over long periods of time without losing control of their drinking. These excessive drinkers are still able to stop after a single drink, although they rarely wish to cease so soon. Excessive drinkers have continued such patterns of drinking for twenty-five years and more without losing control. These heavy drinkers are definitely problems for society, but they are not alcoholics unless they lose control of their drinking. It is an error to regard all heavy drinkers as alcoholics.

The drinker becomes an alcoholic when he suffers loss of control. In the early stages of alcoholism he can refuse to drink, but he cannot stop drinking once he has started. Loss of control means that *after* the consumption of *any amount* of alcohol *in any form* a physical reaction occurs in which a *demand* for alcohol arises, and the demand continues until advanced stages of intoxication make further consumption impossible.

EVOLUTION OF THE ALCOHOLIC

Even during the earliest stages of alcoholism the drinker feels guilty. The alcoholic does not need any sermon to make him feel guilty. His loss of control over drinking disturbs him and produces remorse and defensiveness. Alibis are devised to explain his drinking, but the explanations are directed more to himself even than to family and friends. He attempts to rationalize his drinking by telling why he got drunk and why he will not get drunk again. He changes his drinking habits and may change his geographic location. But he is not able to regain control of drinking.

Reproof from family usually arouses defensive and aggressive reactions as alcoholism progresses. Persistent remorse dominates the alcoholic, however, and he regularly climbs on the water wagon, swearing never to drink again. His failures become so embarrassing that he withdraws from old friends, frequently because he fears that they are ready to withdraw friendship from him.

A point of shock in the evolution of the alcoholic is the first loss of job due to uncontrolled drinking. Up to this point the alcoholic has worried about how his drinking affects his activities. From now on concentrated efforts are made to prevent other activities from interfering with his drinking. The family changes its habits, attempting to shield the alcoholic. In his lonely drinking he harbors deep resentments and becomes hypercritical of everyone.

The morning "eye opener" drink "to start the day right" becomes a necessity. It not only helps to alleviate the pain of the hangover, but it helps quiet the feelings of guilt and remorse. The morning drink seems "medicine."

The morning drink does not produce sufficient effect for long. The alcoholic at long last turns to doctors or hospitals for help. He may go to a psychiatrist or a clergyman. Many times he is pushed by his spouse to seek help. All too often, however, he receives no lasting benefit. He is unwilling to persist in his attempts to find help. He refuses to admit the extent of his drinking or the seriousness of his problems.

LATE-STAGE ALCOHOLISM

The alcoholic enters the chronic phase of alcoholism or late-stage alcoholism with the advent of the first bender. He drinks for days at a time. He disregards everything as he gets helplessly drunk. Family, job, food, clothing, and housing no longer seem important. He drinks to escape problems caused by drinking—and creates new problems from which he must try to escape by more drinking.

Until the alcoholic reached the bender stage, he could choose whether he would drink or not, even though he could not stop drinking once he chose to drink. Now all choice and control are gone. The alcoholic now drinks as much and as frequently as he can. He lives to drink so that he can forget that he lives.

Ethical deterioration sets in rapidly in the advanced stages of alcoholism. Coupled with this deterioration is a constant obsession with fears and anxieties, many of them indefinable. Doom and destruction seem imminent. Extreme nervousness will respond only to alcoholic dosage. A nervous condition commonly called the "shakes" upsets him. Such simple tasks as the tying of shoe laces often cannot be performed without a drink. After a drink the "shakes" disappear for a while only to return, demanding more alcoholic intake. Alcoholic diseases resulting from nutritional deficiencies often develop. Delirium tremens adds to the nervousness and fears.

Eventually, if he is still alive after all that he has been through, the alcoholic "hits bottom." His alibi system collapses and is no longer capable of fooling anyone, not even himself. In despair and surrender he admits defeat. He seeks help, realizing his inability to stop drinking or to solve his problems without outside assistance. Numerous alcoholics never "hit bottom," never surrender, never respond to therapy. Only as the alibis collapse is the alcoholic able to recover. Often the alcoholic recognizes a deep religious need as he surrenders. Some assert that recovery is dependent upon a recognition of religious need.

The description of the evolution of the alcoholic is derived from work undertaken by Dr. E. M. Jellenik, world renowned authority on alcoholism. The World Health Organization has sponsored the spreading of this knowledge of the developing phases of alcohol addiction. The National Council on Alcoholism has printed and widely distributed data on the typical evolution of alcoholics.

The description does not apply in every detail to every alcoholic. The sequence of details may vary slightly from individual to individual. The results are drawn from observations of large numbers of alcoholics over extended periods. The average alcoholic drinks for about eight years before he suffers loss of control. On the average, he then drinks for about seven more years before he hits bottom. The whole process may be as short as seven years from first drink to the bottom of the skids, or it may run twenty-five years or longer.

The alcoholic follows an irrational course to an unhappy state. The compulsive character of his disorder seems obvious. He can be declared a sick man. But of what type is his sickness? Does he have disease? Is his trouble chiefly physical? Or, are the physical ailments symptomatic of mental disturbances?

CAUSES OF ALCOHOLISM

There are no conclusive answers to the nature of the alcoholic disability. Advocates can be found who trace the cause of alcoholism to physiological grounds. Others believe the root of the whole problem can be found in the psychological make-up of the alcoholic. Proponents of various combinations of these two extreme positions also suggest theories of causation. Each theory has related research which seems to corroborate the theory. More research is needed—more money is needed to make such research possible. It is to be hoped that future research will help us to understand more about the causes of alcoholism. An understanding of causation may hasten the development of better therapy for the alcoholic.

Currently the psychological theories of causation of alcoholism are most widely held. The alcoholic person is frequently pictured as immature and arrested in interpersonal relations. Alcoholism is a pattern of adjustment to developing stress and strain. According to this theory, alcoholism is a symptom of a maladjustment in personality. It is not the real problem, but is the visible demonstration of the underlying problem. Any solution of the problem of alcoholism is looked upon as only partial unless it involves therapy for the underlying problems also. This theory has much to recommend it. The many authorities in the field who hold this view influence the novice and nonprofessional person to trust that the psychological theory is the best theory so far advanced.

An incipient psychological weakness may or may not underlie alcoholism. It cannot be said with certainty that the psychological weakness preceded the first use of alcohol. It is not questioned, however, that the use of alcohol by an alcoholic produces psychological maladjustments. Alcohol is the catalyst which produces a vicious circle of harmful personal reactions.

Abraham Myerson, among others, claims "that social tradition and social pressure are all-important factors in the genesis of alcoholism, in addition to whatever personal difficulty or personal disability harasses the individual." [1] He accepts the psychological weaknesses of the popular theories. He asks, however, for the reasons for the differential rates between men and women, between Gentile and Jew, and between other varying groups. He reminds us that there are seven or eight male alcoholics to each female alcoholic in our society. He makes the point that alcoholism is very rare among Jewish people. Do not women have as much stress and strain as men? Do not Jews meet with as many difficulties of adjusting to society as do Gentiles? Are not there as many neurotic and disturbed women

---

[1] Quoted in McCarthy, *op. cit.*, p. 310.

as men? Are not Jews as troubled by frustration, insecurity, and anxiety as are Gentiles? Since the answers to all these questions are assumed to be affirmative, why are not the rates of incidence of alcoholism similar?

Most of the advocates of physiological causation of alcoholism are European scholars. Although their current answers seem inadequate, future research may cause revision of all current theories. All research into the nature of alcoholism should be encouraged.

PHYSIOLOGICAL EFFECTS

It is well known and accepted by medical authorities that alcoholism does produce serious bodily ailments. The diseases or ailments most common among chronic alcoholics are chiefly nutritional diseases. They arise from the nature of alcohol as a source of bodily energy and the effect of drinking it upon eating habits.

The basic nutritional elements needed by the body are proteins, carbohydrates, fats, minerals, and vitamins. Through metabolism these elements are converted into energy and nutrients for the body. The energy component of food is measured in calories.

When more calories are taken into the body through food than are burned up in activity, the surplus is stored in the tissues as fat or sugar. This surplus may be drawn upon later as needed. Alcohol is a rich source of calories, but contains no nutrients. An ounce of alcohol contains about 200 calories. A pint of whiskey furnishes about 1,400 calories—almost half the daily needs of a man. But calories in alcohol cannot be stored in the tissues; they must be burned.

The alcoholic who consumes as much as a pint of whiskey per day over any lengthy period comes to rely more and more upon alcohol to meet his energy requirements. His appetite decreases. He may eat less than half as much food as his body needs. Although he has plenty of energy, he is lacking in nutrients. The digestive organs may become irritated from the high alcoholic content of the diet. These irritations prevent the complete absorption of such vitamins and minerals as are eaten by the alcoholic. Nutritional diseases develop from poor eating habits brought on by the heavy drinking of alcohol.

Beriberi and pellagra are two vitamin deficiency diseases arising from improper eating habits among alcoholics. Beriberi "is characterized by a degeneration of the peripheral nerves sometimes accompanied by circulatory disturbances (heart disease) and generalized dropsy. In severe states of deficiency the patient experiences difficulty in walking; paralysis of the arms and eye muscles may appear, with associated clouding of consciousness and possible brain damage." [2] Pellagra results in "inflammation of the skin, irrations of the mouth, gastrointestinal disturbances, and mental illness. In cases of severe acute deficiency there may be fever and stupor, culminating in death." [3]

Cirrhosis of the liver has long been known as a drinking man's ailment. The old theories were wrong in assuming that liquor had a direct effect upon the liver. Cirrhosis is a disease that afflicts many, including children and teetotalers. The incidence of cirrhosis is eight times as high for alcoholics, however, as for the general population. Cirrhosis prevents the body from using all the food elements taken into the body. Cirrhosis may produce death. Cirrhosis is a common, serious disease of the alcoholic, affecting his absorption of nutritional elements at a time when he already is getting too few vitamins and minerals.

Weakened by nutritional diseases and poor dietary habits, the alcoholic is more susceptible to many common ailments. Alcoholism is a contributing factor in many deaths attributed to malnutrition, tuberculosis, and heart disorders. Alcoholics constitute a serious health problem, physically and psychologically, for our nation.

---

[2] McCarthy and Douglass, *op. cit.*, p. 94.

[3] *Ibid.*, p. 95.

A MOST SERIOUS HEALTH PROBLEM

The seriousness of alcoholism as a health problem is admitted. It is one of the ten most serious health problems in the nation. If the importance of the problem is determined from the number who suffer from the ailment, then alcoholism rates as the fourth most serious health problem. The mayor of San Francisco in a public address labeled alcoholism the number one health problem of his city.

The most recent data for alcoholics in the United States estimate the number of alcoholics for 1956. In that year there were 5,015,000 alcoholics in the United States. Male alcoholics outnumbered females by a ratio of five and a half to one.

There has been a substantial increase in number of alcoholics in the last decade. Some of the increase is due to the increase of the adult population of the nation. There has been a sharp increase in the rate of alcoholism also, but not as rapid as the increase in numbers. In 1956 there were 4,760 alcoholics for every 100,000 adults in the population. In 1946 the rate was 3,330 alcoholics per 100,000 adults. These data indicate, therefore, that the rate of alcoholism increased by 43 per cent in the most recent decade for which figures are available.

INCREASE IN NUMBER OF ALCOHOLICS

1945   (2,876,000)

1950   (5,015,000)

Each Symbol Represents 500,000 Persons

55

The rate of alcoholism is now lower, even with recent increases, than it was in 1910. The 1956 rate is 75 per cent higher than the rate for 1920 and 78 per cent higher than the rate for 1930. A high rate of alcoholism prevailed prior to World War I and the enactment of the Eighteenth Amendment. The lowest rates of alcoholism were reached during the period when the Eighteenth Amendment was a part of the law of the nation. Since 1930 the rate has steadily increased to the point that it is now approaching the highest rate ever attained.

TABLE 1

ESTIMATED NUMBERS OF ALCOHOLICS AND RATES OF ALCOHOLISM IN THE UNITED STATES, 1910-1956, BY SEX

	MALES		FEMALES		TOTAL	
	Number	Rate	Number	Rate	Number	Rate
1910	2,281,000	8,180	392,000	1,540	2,673,000	4,990
1920	1,441,000	4,470	270,000	890	1,711,000	2,720
1930	1,699,000	4,460	320,000	860	2,018,000	2,680
1940	2,256,000	5,230	376,000	870	2,632,000	3,050
1945	2,432,000	5,290	444,000	950	2,876,000	3,090
1950	3,280,000	6,710	596,000	1,180	3,876,000	3,890
1955	4,002,000	7,860	710,000	1,330	4,712,000	4,520
1956	4,243,000	8,270	772,000	1,430	5,015,000	4,760

Source: Yale University Center of Alcohol Studies, Mark Keller and Vera Efron

The rates of alcoholism vary widely within the nation. A most commonly remarked difference in rates occurs between urban and rural areas, with urban areas having the higher incidence of alcoholics. States selling liquor by the drink rather than by the package also have higher rates of alcoholism. In the data for 1955 California had the highest alcoholic rate—6,600 per 100,000 adults. In the same year Wyoming had the lowest rate—1,510. Fourteen states had rates higher than the national average, while thirty-four states had rates lower.[4]

---

[4] Mark Keller and Vera Efron, "The Rate of Alcoholism in the U.S.A., 1954-1956," *Quarterly Journal of Studies on Alcohol*, Vol. XIX, No. 2, June 1958, Table III, pp. 317-8.

Recent data for cities are available only for alcoholics with complications. In 1950 San Francisco led the nation with a rate of 4,190 chronic alcoholics per 100,000 adult population. Sacramento, California, the second city, is far behind with a rate of 2,780. Louisville and San Diego rank third and fourth, respectively.[5]

These wide variations in rate of alcoholism from state to state and from city to city give rise to questions. What lies back of these variations? What factors in San Francisco are responsible for the greater prevalence of alcoholism? Is either the social environment or the physical environment a conditioning factor partially responsible for the greater incidence of alcoholism? Answers to these questions could well yield important clues for a program of prevention of alcoholism.

AN INTERNATIONAL HEALTH PROBLEM

These very same questions arise as we note the differences in rates of alcoholism from country to country. The data which compare countries are not as accurate as those for this nation alone; the data are gathered for different years and reflect differences in methods of reporting causes of deaths.

These data for the various countries of the world are far more accurate for the number of alcoholics with complications than for the total of all alcoholics. The total number of alcoholics reported for Chile, Italy, and England and Wales is probably much too low in each instance.

In a comparison of chronic alcoholics the United States ranks fourth. The use of data for 1946 or 1947 for the United States would not change its rank order. Chronic alcoholism is a more serious problem in Switzerland, Chile, and France than in this country. Recent unofficial estimates indicate that France now has the highest rate of chronic alcoholism of any nation. In the period from 1946 to 1956 the rate of deaths attributed to

[5] Mark Keller and Vera Efron, "Alcoholism in the Big Cities of the United States," *Quarterly Journal of Studies on Alcohol*, Vol. XVII, March 1956, p. 68.

TABLE 2

ESTIMATED RATES OF ALCOHOLISM IN VARIOUS COUNTRIES

Country	Year	With Complications	With and Without Complications
Switzerland	1947	1,590	2,385
Chile	1946	1,497	1,500
France	1945	1,420	2,850
U. S. A.	1956	1,190	4,760
Australia	1947	671	1,340
Sweden	1946	646	2,580
Denmark	1948	487	1,950
Italy	1942	476	500
Canada	1952	407	1,630
Norway	1947	389	1,560
Finland	1947	357	1,430
England and Wales	1948	278	1,100

Sources: United States from Yale University Center of Alcohol Studies; Canada from R. J. Gibbins, *Alcoholism in Canada*: all other countries from World Health Organization, Expert Committee on Mental Health.

delirium tremens and alcoholically induced insanity increased by 1,167 per cent.[6]

In a comparison of total alcoholics the United States ranks first in the world. The use of data from an earlier year would not change this rank order. This position of pre-eminence among the nations stirs no pride in us. Although we as American citizens do pride ourselves on the quality and availability of medical care, we still lead the world in incidence of alcoholism.

Although alcoholism has been a serious problem in this nation for a long time, it is only recently that it has been treated as a health problem. Treatment for the alcoholic has too often consisted only of confinement to a jail. In colonial America alcoholics were placed in stocks in the public square. Disgust and

---

[6] *New York Times*, August 4, 1957.

contempt, anger and hostility, shame and fear were the attitudes most commonly accorded the alcoholic. The family and friends of the alcoholic cooperated to conceal the alcoholic's condition from the public.

All the churches have regarded drunkenness as sinful. Since the alcoholic was frequently drunk, he was regarded as a moral outcast. The alcoholic was either ignored by the church or harassed by exhortations urging him to use his will and give up drinking. Neither course of action has been very helpful.

During the past fifteen years there have developed in the nation different attitudes toward the alcoholic. Many persons have begun to regard the alcoholic with greater objectivity and less emotion. Some of the stigma has been removed.

Two organizations have been most instrumental in producing the changing attitudes toward the alcoholic: Alcoholics Anonymous and the Yale Center of Alcohol Studies. Each of these organizations has accomplished much in a short time.

THE YALE CENTER

The Yale Center developed as a division of the Laboratory of Applied Physiology of Yale University. Separate studies on alcohol were instituted in 1930 and 1931. It was soon found that the problems of alcohol cut across the lines of academic discipline. A new cooperative approach was decided upon which would utilize the knowledge and services of psychologists, lawyers, educators, sociologists as well as physiologists. Research is the basic work of the Yale Center.

The Yale Center has been interested in the practical utility of its research. Information about all phases of alcohol education is published in the *Quarterly Journal of Studies on Alcohol.* A master bibliography on all scientific studies concerning alcohol is maintained. Both of these projects began in 1939. In 1943 the Yale Summer School of Alcohol Studies was instituted. These activities help representatives of industry, education, government, social welfare services, and religion keep well informed about the latest findings relative to alcohol.

A major concern of the Yale Center has been alcoholism. The Center has not only fostered education concerning alcoholism, but has also initiated treatment centers. The first Yale Plan Clinic was established in 1943. The clinics have served as models for many of the institutions established by state commissions on alcoholism. State commissions on alcoholism, state boards of education, and some church groups have come to rely upon the Yale Center for guidance and assistance in their programs of prevention of alcoholism.

ALCOHOLICS ANONYMOUS

Alcoholics Anonymous is an organization with a much more narrowly defined goal than the Yale Center. The goal of A. A. is the rehabilitation of alcoholics. This organization has been more successful in assisting alcoholics than any other agency. The simple statement of purpose covers well the activities of the movement: "Alcoholics Anonymous is a fellowship of men and women who share their experience, strength, and hope with each other that they may solve their common problem and help others to recover from alcoholism. The only requirement for membership is a desire to stop drinking. There are no dues or fees for A. A. membership; we are self-supporting through our own contributions. A. A. is not allied with any sect, denomination, politics, organization, or institution; does not wish to engage in any controversy, neither endorses nor opposes any causes. Our primary purpose is to stay sober and help other alcoholics to achieve sobriety."

A. A. is unique in that its membership is composed of alcoholics. It was organized by two alcoholics in 1935 in Akron, Ohio. Utilizing ideas and techniques drawn from various other movements, these two men wrestled with their alcoholism by assisting other alcoholics. Soon the movement had spread to Cleveland, Chicago, Philadelphia, Los Angeles, Washington, and New York. Within six years about 2,000 men and women were active in the A. A. program.

In 1941 A. A. received its first major national publicity. An article in the *Saturday Evening Post* by Jack Alexander aroused interest across the country. Alcoholics and the families of alcoholics found a first ray of hope in this story. Chapters were founded in hundreds of communities. The movement became world-wide with groups in fifty countries. It is estimated that there are now more than 250,000 members meeting regularly in more than 8,000 groups.

Alcoholics Anonymous—commonly referred to in A. A. as "the big book"—was written by the two founders of the movement. This book is still in print and is still the standard reference book for the alcoholic seeking help. Many pamphlets and a periodical, *The A. A. Grapevine,* regularly spread the good news of possible rehabilitation to the alcoholic.

A. A. is very loosely organized. There are no national officers. Fifteen trustees maintain a New York center for production and dissemination of literature. All expenses are met through gifts of members of A. A. No gifts from outside sources are received, although many have been offered.

The A. A. group includes within its fellowship representatives of the various strata of society. Professional men and unskilled laborers work together to achieve sobriety. Men and women belong to the same group, seeking solutions for the common ailment. The group may be so small as to include only two alcoholics, but there is no limit to the number that may belong to a group. It has been found through experience that a group numbering from twenty-five to fifty is most effective.

In weekly closed meetings the members discuss their problems. This closed meeting may be led by a specialist speaking on some phase of the problem of alcoholism. It usually consists of the telling of experiences by the members. These experience meetings frequently remind one of religious services and "testimonies" as practiced within some churches.

Open meetings are held frequently. The public is invited to these meetings to hear the members talk about alcoholism. The open meetings educate the public and secure new members.

The A. A. group often meets in a church. Other public meeting places are also common meeting places. A church or other organization is never allowed to sponsor A. A., however. Some churches have resented the unwillingness of A. A. to affiliate with a church. Others have reacted against the A. A. tradition of refusing to adopt a policy on total abstinence or legislative control. The churches need to realize that A. A. does not enter into controversy. The alcoholic is a sick person, and he has enough troubles without getting into controversy.

The success of the A. A. program has derived from the warmth and understanding extended to an alcoholic by another alcoholic. Bill W., one of the founders of A. A., declares that there is not a single new fundamental in the program of A. A. He attributes the success to the creation of a society in which the alcoholic can use principles of psychiatry and religion. These principles are the widely publicized and greatly esteemed suggested twelve steps to recovery.

TWELVE STEPS TO RECOVERY

These twelve steps were first printed in "the big book"— *Alcoholics Anonymous*—but are now available in a variety of formats. A favorite form of printing consists of a card to be carried in a billfold. These twelve steps are as follows:

1—We admitted we were powerless over alcohol—that our lives had become unmanageable.
2—Came to believe that a Power greater than ourselves could restore us to sanity.
3—Made a decision to turn our will and our lives over to the care of God as we understood Him.
4—Made a searching and fearless moral inventory of ourselves.

5—Admitted to God, to ourselves and to another human being the exact nature of our wrongs.

6—Were entirely ready to have God remove all these defects of character.

7—Humbly asked Him to remove our shortcomings.

8—Made a list of all persons we had harmed, and became willing to make amends to them all.

9—Made direct amends to such people wherever possible, except when to do so would injure them or others.

10—Continued to take personal inventory and when we were wrong, promptly admitted it.

11—Sought through prayer and meditation to improve our conscious contact with God as we understood Him, praying only for knowledge of His will for us and the power to carry that out.

12—Having had a spiritual awakening as the result of these steps, we tried to carry this message to alcoholics and practice these principles in all our affairs.

The religious element is clearly evident in these twelve steps. The religion is not sectarian and may even be non-Christian. Usually it is Christian, however. Clergymen are generally welcomed to A. A., although members may argue with the clergyman over his concepts of God. No member of A.A. is required to believe in God—or even the twelve steps or any other item of the program—but within a year's time from entry into A. A. nearly every member has a religious orientation. Bill W. asserts: "I know scarcely an A. A. member of more than a year's standing who still thinks his transformation wholly a psychological phenomenon based entirely upon his own normal resources. Almost everyone of our members will tell you that . . . he has developed [a concept of God] of his own on which he can positively depend." [7]

In numerous situations the clergyman is welcomed as one

---

[7] Bill W., *Alcoholism the Illness,* New York: Alcoholics Anonymous, 1950, p. 10.

who can assist in the work of the fifth step. The clergyman may fulfill this step by counseling or by hearing confession. Not every clergyman is prepared, either through interest or training, to perform fifth step work. The interested minister usually finds many who need his spiritual guidance.

The member of A. A. usually finds that the first step is hardest. He does not really believe at first that he is powerless over alcohol. A. A. explains that many relapses occur because the new member is not thoroughly convinced of his inability to control alcohol. The first step is also made difficult by well-meaning friends and relatives who tell the alcoholic that he is not an alcoholic. These friends probably consider alcoholism a disgrace, or hold inaccurate stereotypes of the alcoholic, or feel threatened in their own drinking habits. Even ministers may hinder the alcoholic from taking the first step by their admonitions that the drinker exercise his will power and stop drinking.

The alcoholic finds that the other eleven steps follow naturally and logically from the first step. The twelfth step is a step of service to others in need, but it reinforces the alcoholic in his efforts to remain sober.

The A. A. member will do anything possible to help another alcoholic and prevent him from drinking. He will arise at any hour of the night and go at a moment's notice to help an alcoholic wrestle with the urge to drink. The sober alcoholic can do more good in this hour of testing than can one who does not understand the force of the demand for alcohol. The alcoholic is far more apt to be sympathetic when relapses occur. In A. A. one is not censured when he falls from sobriety, but helping hands are extended to effect recovery.

For many alcoholics the prospect of trying to refrain from drinking for the rest of one's life seems overwhelming. It has been found from experience that the alcoholic must, at least at first, think of goals in terms of daily achievements. Ten maxims are listed under the heading "Just for Today," the first of which reads: "Just for today I will try to live through this day only, not to tackle my whole life problem at once. I can do things for 12 hours that would appall me if I had to keep them up for a lifetime." These maxims are also printed on a card to be carried in the billfold.

CHANGES IN A. A.

In the early years of A. A. the members were largely older persons. Few members were less than fifty years of age. Due to education about alcoholism many younger persons are now recognizing their difficulty. A. A. now has members who are in their 30's and 40's, and a few who are younger.

The National Council on Alcoholism is an agency which has achieved much in the education of the general population concerning alcoholism. This organization has widely publicized the early symptoms of alcoholism. Knowledge of these early symptoms has aided diagnosis and referral of alcoholics to A. A. at younger age than seemed possible a decade ago.

In the early years of A. A. many churchmen were dubious or unfriendly to the new movement. The doubts and fears have been removed for the most part. Only an occasional churchman today questions the motives or techniques of A. A. Many outsiders question some of the theories of A. A., but largely waive their questions in consideration of the significant results achieved by the group. Only rarely does a clergyman attempt to help an alcoholic without assistance from A. A.

FAMILIES OF ALCOHOLICS

A. A. was among the first agencies to recognize the problems arising *from* the spouse of the alcoholic. Ministers, social workers, and doctors had long known the problems of the family of the alcoholic stemming from the alcoholism. Pity for the family usually resulted in the alcoholic's being blamed for all discord within the family. All solutions were to derive simply from stopping the drinking. A. A. saw that many family problems could not be solved by sobriety alone. Also, many alcoholics

65

would be unable to remain sober without a change in the spouse.

A subsidiary group for the families of alcoholics cooperates with A. A. This group, called AlAnon, meets weekly as does A. A. The members discuss their problems in much the same manner as do the members of A. A. The AlAnon member usually joins after the family member has been in A. A. for some time and has begun to achieve demonstrable results. Many of them come from curiosity. A few come who have not yet succeeded in getting the alcoholic member of the family to seek any form of help.

AlAnon does help the alcoholic by helping his family members. The family members are often surprised to find that the group does not engage in self-pity. " 'I was quite put out at my first meeting,' one wife said. 'I expected to hear my husband's problem discussed, but there was hardly any mention of husbands. Instead we were invited to examine ourselves. I was huffed when one wife expressed the opinion that fear, worry, gossip, criticism, grudge-bearing, self-righteousness, and self-pity might be as reprehensible as drunkenness, lying, and thieving. This was a shock—it hit home.' " [8]

Yet another subsidiary group called AlAteen has been formed recently. This is an organization of teen-age children of alcoholics. The need for this organization is somewhat similar to the need for AlAnon, but definitely more limited. The teen-agers need to know that there are other youngsters who have problems similar to their own. This group may be quite valuable in the prevention of alcoholism, although the group is so new that no evaluation of it along this line is yet possible. It has been claimed that "from forty to sixty per cent of all alcoholics come from the disturbed background of an alcoholic family." [9] The same authority has also pointed out that many women who marry alcoholics are the daughters of alcoholic fathers.[10] If

---

[8] Jerome Ellison, "Help for the Alcoholic's Family," *Saturday Evening Post,* July 2, 1955, p. 19.

[9] Victor W. Eisenstein, ed., *Neurotic Interaction in Marriage,* New York: Basic Books, Inc., 1956, p. 156.

[10] *Ibid.,* p. 159.

these children of alcoholics can be assisted early, then the future rate of alcoholism may be substantially lowered.

Dr. Ruth Fox, Medical Director of the National Council on Alcoholism, tells of women who marry a succession of alcoholics. Many counselors have noted the same phenomenon. Alcoholism may produce neuroticism throughout the family members. Neurotic persons, on the other hand, may marry alcoholics. In either case the entire family needs assistance if the alcoholic is to recover.

A widely reprinted bit of literature for the wife of the alcoholic is "Do's and Don'ts for the Wives of Alcoholics," originally printed in *Inventory*. This document warns the wife against martyr-like attitudes. The full list is worth repetition because it attacks attitudes held by many:

DO learn the facts about alcoholism.
DO develop an attitude to match the facts.
DO talk to someone who understands alcoholism.
DO take a personal inventory of yourself.
DO go to a clinic or A. A. or AlAnon.
DO maintain a healthy atmosphere in your home.
DO encourage your husband's new interests.
DO take a relapse lightly if there is one.
DO pass your knowledge of alcoholism on to others.

DON'T preach and lecture to your husband.
DON'T have a "holier-than-thou" attitude.
DON'T use the "if you loved me" appeal.
DON'T make threats you won't carry out.
DON'T hide his liquor or pour it out.
DON'T argue with him when he is drunk.
DON'T make an issue over his treatment.
DON'T expect an immediate, 100% recovery.
DON'T be jealous of his method of recovery.
DON'T try to protect him against alcohol.

PUBLIC AGENCIES AND ALCOHOLISM

In an increasing number of regions A. A. now has assistance from public agencies which have programs for therapy for alcoholics. State commissions on alcoholism are being established regularly. These commissions carry on educational programs and establish clinics for the treatment of alcoholics. In some states the alcoholic is treated in the hospitals for mental illness.

Clinics and hospitals use various methods of treatment. The hospitals and clinics begin with thorough diagnosis of the patient's ailments, both physical and psychological. After the diagnosis, a chemical such as disulfuram* may be prescribed. Disulfuram is taken daily as a medication. When taken regularly, drinking is not apt to occur. Anyone who drinks even a small portion of alcohol after dosage of disulfuram becomes violently ill. The fear of the results of drinking prevents drinking while dosage continues.

Clinics and hospitals use both group and individual psychotherapy in the treatment of alcoholics. Psychiatry can help many alcoholics. The outstanding clinics also seek to provide economic rehabilitation of the alcoholic.

CHURCHES AND REHABILITATION

The establishment of clinics and commissions on alcoholism is indicative of the widespread concern of the public over this serious problem. The church must show that it is interested in the rehabilitation of alcoholics. In 1945 certain religious groups were criticized: "With only a few notable exceptions prohibition organizations now oppose the rehabilitation of the alcoholic. To take him off the street and hide him from public eyes in clinics, to rehabilitate him would be—so it is held—entirely to the benefit of the liquor trade." [11] Since that date many major church groups have gone on record in favor of rehabilitation programs.

---

* Sold under the proprietary name Antabuse.
[11] McCarthy, *op. cit.*, p. 341.

The various denominations have prepared excellent materials recently for the use of local churches which wish to assist in the rehabilitation of alcoholics. The Protestant Episcopal Church and The Methodist Church have produced the more detailed plans. The details of the program of The Methodist Church will be considered in a later chapter.

The church need never provide a total program for the rehabilitation of the alcoholic. It must consider that it is one of the several agencies working for the recovery of the problem drinker. It must, therefore, use other facilities as they are available. It has been suggested by Dr. G. Aiken Taylor, Presbyterian minister, that anyone wishing to help an alcoholic should have the following information at his finger tips: 1. The name and address of at least one doctor who is familiar with chronic alcoholism; 2. The address and telephone number of the nearest A. A. group; and, 3. The address and rules for admission of the nearest institution treating alcoholics.[12]

Doctors, A. A., and clinics are all important in the recovery of alcoholics. So, too, are the churches. It has been stated often that no alcoholic has much chance of a permanent recovery unless he solves his spiritual problems. In the church the alcoholic can find the religious orientation of life that will hasten his complete recovery. As he discovers that it is God upon whom he depends through Jesus Christ for grace to stop drinking, he can find that the love of God is freely given him. He can find the full meaning of surrender and humility as proper responses to the love of God. (Dr. Harry Tiebout holds that surrender and humility are necessary for the recovery of the alcoholic.[13]) He can find in the church a fellowship that strengthens and heals.

---

[12] "You Can Help the Alcoholic," *Christianity Today*, Vol. II, No. 20, July 7, 1958, p. 10. *Counseling the Alcoholic,* by Howard J. Clinebell, Jr., Abingdon Press, 1956, is a recommended source for additional help at this point.

[13] Treatment of Alcohol Addiction," *Quarterly Journal of Studies on Alcohol*, Vol. V, pp. 84-85.

A Summary Comparison of
Using Alcohol in Bible Times and Today

In Bible Times	*Today*
Wine had a place as a food and beverage since water and milk were often unsafe to drink.	Modern sanitation and refrigeration make unnecessary our reliance on wine as a safe beverage.
Wine had an alcoholic content of only 14 or 15 per cent.	Alcoholic beverages today have an alcoholic content as high as 50 per cent.
Intoxication was the chief ill-effect from drinking, and it did not occur unless as much as 1 quart of wine was drunk (without food).	Drinking small amounts of alcohol can be dangerous—for example, in reducing self-control and in driving ability.
The production of wine was a normal (and limited) part of an agricultural economy. Each family produced its own wine.	The manufacture of liquor is a part of a highly organized business operation, seeking to make as much profit as possible from sales.
Drinking was a family practice, set within the normal restraints of family mores. It was engaged in as a friendly, leisurely social practice.	Drinking may be in family settings, but a large part occurs in bars and taverns and at parties and dinners, where family and other restraining mores do not operate. In addition, other factors operate to encourage drinking for its own sake; modern advertising seeks to create a demand for the use of alcoholic beverages.
Drunkenness in a simple, slowly moving, agricultural economy was harmful chiefly to the drinker and those immediately dependent on him.	Drunkenness—even minor drinking—in our highly industrialized and mechanized society has come to have a new seriousness for all our people. A slow or false reaction by an engineer or pilot may jeopardize the lives of hundreds.

CHAPTER IV

Alcohol and the Bible

BY tradition Protestants turn first to the Bible for ethical insights with which to meet any problem, social or personal. For many Protestants the Bible is the only valid source of ethical insight. Although other Protestants do not regard the Bible as the *sole* source of religious guidance, all Protestants regard the Bible as of primary importance in revealing the ethical insights by which the Christian life is to be governed.

Christians should read the Bible without preconceived notions as to what they will find in the Scriptures. An open mind should be brought to the study of the Bible.

Many Protestant Christians study the Bible to find support of their views on alcohol. They come to the study of the Scriptures with preconceived notions. They are sure that any use of alcoholic beverages is wrong. They conclude that the Bible must, therefore, condemn the use of alcohol.

The Bible does not, however, always condemn the use of wine. It does always condemn *excessive* use of wine, but the *moderate* use of wine is seldom condemned. The Biblical attitudes toward wine must be interpreted in the light of the conditions prevailing during Biblical times. The Bible contains many detailed rules, but often the rules are not applicable to modern-day living. The insights underlying the rules furnish the bases of contemporary Christian living.

Some believers in abstinence from the use of alcohol have frequently gone back to the original Hebrew and Greek languages in which the Scriptures were written. They hope to find in the different words translated "wine" some distinctions in meaning. Perhaps, they hope, the use of grape juice is allowed, but the use of fermented grape juice is not allowed. Such claims are still made, but there is little support for these views.

71

OLD TESTAMENT TRUTHS

The Hebrew word most commonly used for wine is *yayin*. This Hebrew word is used about 140 times in the Old Testament. All agree that this word refers to fermented wine. Noah drank *yayin* and was intoxicated. (Genesis 9:20-21.) Lot drank *yayin* and was intoxicated. (Genesis 19:32-35.) Drunkenness from the use of *yayin* was condemned in various passages in the Old Testament (Proverbs 20:1, 23:29-32; Isaiah 28:1-7; Habakkuk 2:5).

The use of *yayin* is not always condemned in the Old Testament. A great passage from Isaiah reads: "Ho, every one who thirsts, come to the waters; and he who has no money, come, buy and eat; come, buy *yayin* and milk without money and without price" (55:1). In Psalm 104:14 God is praised for the gift of *yayin*.

Next to *yayin* the word *tirosh* is most commonly used in the Old Testament. This word refers to grape juice in the various stages of fermentation. It may refer to grapes in the vat as well as to the pressed juice. *Tirosh* is often translated "new wine," but this does not mean that *tirosh* is always unfermented.

Hosea couples *tirosh* with bad company in proclaiming: "Harlotry and *yayin* and *tirosh* take away the understanding" (4:11). The Jewish law in the Talmud levies a tax on *tirosh* from the first appearance of scum. The appearance of scum on grape juice occurs only when fermentation has occurred.

Some advocates of abstinence assert that *tirosh* always refers to unfermented grape juice. No reputable commentary will allow such usage. An examination of these two common words for wine lends no support to the teaching of abstinence.

The other Hebrew words for wine are not commonly used. No one of them can be used to mean unfermented juice. All of the Hebrew words for wine show an indifference to distinctions between fermented and unfermented. It is not at all surprising that no such distinctions should prevail. Refrigeration was unknown in Palestine in Biblical times. The hot weather rapidly produced fermentation. Some authorities even doubt that *tirosh* could ever mean unfermented grape juice because the climatic conditions would have made unfermented juice impossible. It can definitely be said that unfermented juice was quite rare.

Wine was regarded as a necessity by the people of the Old Testament. It was a common beverage and was regarded as a food (Lamentations 2:12; Zechariah 9:17; Judges 19:19; I Samuel 16:20; 25:18). It was used as a medicine and a drug. A fine wine year was regarded as a special blessing from God (Genesis 27:28; Deuteronomy 7:13; Amos 9:13-14; Joel 3:18). Wine was always to be regarded as a gift of God and as a symbol of all gifts of God. Its use in ritual stemmed from this symbolic meaning.

Wine was also condemned on occasion. Drunkenness was always condemned. The prominent persons who became intoxicated included Noah, Lot, Nabal, Uriah, Elah, Ammon, and Benhadad. This list indicates that the problem of drunkenness was of importance. Evidently women also became intoxicated (I Samuel 1:13; Amos 6:6, 4:1). It is likely that drunkenness was ordinarily a vice of the wealthy.

The Old Testament describes well the results of intoxication. It lists staggering, uncertain gait, vomiting, incoherent speech, unnecessary wounds, red eyes, double vision, laughing without reason, insensitivity, dizziness, and a drinking habit (Job 12:35; Psalms 107:27; Proverbs 23:29, 33; Isaiah 28:7; Genesis 43:34; Ecclesiastes 30:40; Jeremiah 51:39, 57; Psalms 77:65; Ecclesiastes 37:34). The mind of the intoxicated man is pictured as blunted in conscience, weakened in will, forgetful, and incapable of exercising good judgment (Isaiah 28:7; Hosea 4:11). He keeps bad company and will be attracted to lust (Joel 3:3; Ecclesiastes 31:26, 29). Drunkenness turns a man away from God and religion (Isaiah 5:12).

In the Old Testament there were two groups of abstainers: Nazirites and Rechabites. Neither of these groups was very numerous nor particularly highly regarded.

73

The Nazirites took a threefold vow, one part of which required abstinence from wine and all fruits of the vine (Numbers 6:6). The vow was not necessarily a permanent vow. The Nazirite could be released from his vows at the end of a term and return to the use of wine (Numbers 6:10-20). Samson and Samuel have been regarded by some scholars as Nazirites, although the record does not make this clear.

The Rechabites abstained from the use of wine because of their devotion to the nomadic way of life (Jeremiah 33:5; 35:6-7). These deeply religious persons noted the drinking habits of the agricultural Canaanites and opposed them. They believed that God did not want his people to settle down and become agricultural; they could escape the immorality of the Canaanites by remaining nomads.

Neither of these two groups was of any importance in the development of Judaism. Nowhere do the prophets call for the people to follow the example of these abstainers.

The priests were forbidden the use of wine while engaged in the rites of the priestly office (Leviticus 10:9). The later word from Ezekiel seems to indicate that priests were free to drink except when engaged in the holiest of rites (44:21).

The rabbinical writings note that wine was used in the Passover service, in the marriage ceremony, at circumcision, in certain blessings, at grace after meals, and in prayers of mourning. Some rabbis traced wine back to the forbidden fruit in Eden. Many of the world's troubles were traced back to wine. Exact rules and laws were proclaimed governing all circumstances of drinking. These rules were set up to help man use God's gift to make him happy, but also prevent him from falling into disaster through intoxication.

NEW TESTAMENT TEACHINGS

The Hebrew attitudes toward wine generally prevail in the New Testament writings. Surprisingly few references to drinking are to be found in the Gospels. Wine is still regarded as food, drink, medicine, and drug (Luke 7:33; John 2:3; Matthew 26:29; Luke 10:34; Mark 15:23). Wine is used in the Last Supper, although it is not clear whether this was as food or as symbol.

In the New Testament two Greek words are used to refer to wine. *Gleukos* is the Greek equivalent of the Hebrew word which denoted the grape, pressed or in the vat. This is the word that some advocates of abstinence insist refers to an unfermented drink. Such interpretation is unwarranted. At the gift of the Holy Spirit on the day of Pentecost the disciples were mocked by bystanders. They charged the ecstatic behavior of the Christians to drinking: "They are filled with *gleukos*" (Acts 2:13). This evidently referred to intoxication.

The common word in the New Testament for wine is *oinos*. There is no question that this word always refers to an intoxicating beverage. As such, its use is the subject of many warnings. Jesus said of it: "Take heed to yourselves lest your hearts be weighed down with dissipation and drunkenness . . ." (Luke 21:34). In the parable of the evil stewards their wickedness in part consists of drunkenness (Matthew 24:45-51; Luke 12:42-48).

Almost without question Jesus drank wine with meals and as a part of ritual observances. There is little reason to believe that he was a Nazirite. It is likely that John the Baptist was a Nazirite, but Jesus is contrasted sharply in habits from John (Matthew 11:18-19; Luke 7:33-35). Of Jesus it was said: "The Son of man came eating and drinking, and they say, 'Behold a glutton and a drunkard. . . .'" It is recorded in the Fourth Gospel that Jesus changed water into wine at the wedding in Cana (John 2:1-11; 4:16). However we interpret the Cana story, there is no doubt that the early Christians believed that Jesus approved the use of wine at a marriage feast.

Paul had much more to say concerning drinking wine than do the authors of the Gospels. It is quite likely that Paul encountered drunkenness in his travels more frequently than did

Jesus. Paul opposed intemperance but had no harsh view of wine. He included drunkenness in all his lists of the vices (Galatians 5:19-21). It is no accident that he links drunkenness with such bad company. He regarded drunkenness as serious enough to bring separation from the kingdom of God (I Corinthians 6:10).

Paul warns Christians to shun associations with drunkards (I Corinthians 5:11). Drunkenness desecrates the body, the temple of the Holy Spirit, and even injures the whole church (I Corinthians 3:16-17). Particularly distressed at the riotous behavior at love feasts, Paul warned against excesses of drink (I Corinthians 11:21-22). He advised, "Let us conduct ourselves as in the day, not in reveling and drunkenness . . ." (Romans 13:13).

Paul did not absolutely prohibit the use of alcohol. Most of the references he made to wine deal with drunkenness, which he always condemned. He did say, "It is right not to eat meat or drink wine or do anything that makes your brother stumble" (Romans 14:21). This advice rose from a special situation referring to meat or drink offered to idols. The exact details of this advice need not apply to all situations involving meat or drink, but the ethical principle stated here applies to the use of anything which brings offence to a Christian brother.

The pastoral Epistles also showed concern over drunkenness. Bishops and deacons were required to refrain from drinking too much (I Timothy 3:2, 8). Elderly women were warned against becoming slaves of wine (Titus 2:3). Wine is looked upon as having medicinal value as Timothy is advised to use a little wine for his stomach's sake (I Timothy 5:23).

INTERPRETATION OF THE SCRIPTURES

Any consideration of the Biblical teachings about alcohol convinces that intemperance is consistently opposed. Throughout both Old and New Testaments drunkenness is regarded as a sin. Intoxication is pictured as productive of other sins and of many evil consequences. The attitudes of many church-men toward alcoholics arise from the Biblical attitude toward drunkenness. (Of course, there was no understanding of the nature of alcoholism in Biblical times. It is also unlikely that alcoholism was common.)

Any consideration of the full range of the Biblical teachings about alcohol also reveals that the Bible does not furnish proof texts explicitly requiring abstinence for all godly men. Absti-nence under certain conditions is taught, but moderation may be applicable for other situations. It constitutes a misuse of the Scriptures to ignore certain Biblical references because these passages do not support the position of abstinence. It is also a misuse of the Scriptures to ignore other Biblical references which support the limited application of abstinence.

Advocates of moderate drinking use the Bible to support their desires. Many of them condemn as unbiblical those who wish to practice abstinence. Others disapprove attempts to impose abstinence upon all Christians: "Dare he [the min-ister] brand as sinful any participation in any kind of social drinking? There are numbers of clergy who are certain in their own minds that they must. But this certainty is not with the authority of the Scriptures. It is not with the blessing of custom of past ages. It is not consistent with much ethnic practice in predominantly Christian countries. It is not realistic when considered against the background of the prevalent social custom of many of even the 'best' church members." [1]

In the same article Chaplain Wiltenburg writes: "Admoni-tions like this [Isaiah 5:11, 12, 22; 28:7] are manifestly warnings against immoderate use rather than prohibitions of any use of alcohol. Still the prohibitory recommendation is implied and must be seriously considered." [2] He gives no other consideration, however, to implications toward total abstinence as a rule of holiness. Rather social customs and the Christian

W. J. Wiltenburg, "The Bible and the Attitudes of Ministers on Drinking," *Pastoral Psychology*, Vol. IX, No. 83, April 1958, p. 41.
  [2] *Ibid.*, p. 40.

professions of certain nations and certain "best" church members become sufficient reasons for the condemnation of the abstinence position.

Proof texts can be used to "prove" abstinence as the godly way. Different proof texts can be used by others to "prove" that drinking is encouraged by the Bible. The Scriptures neither "prove" nor "disprove" abstinence from alcoholic beverages. The use of proof texts as evidence in this or any other controversy is not recommended. All too frequently the Scriptures are distorted as they are used as proof for a position already assumed.

The Scriptures must be interpreted in the light of the conditions prevailing at the time of writing. The Bible speaks of the needs of the men who first read the writings. The Scriptures still speak to us too, but with modified impact. Many of the writings of Paul to the Greek churches state principles which may still be applied, but the detailed applications advocated by Paul are no longer pertinent to us. Few twentieth-century Christians need worry about eating meat offered to idols, but we need always be concerned that we do not offend our brother by an undue exercise of freedom.

CHANGES FROM THE BIBLICAL WORLD

Science has worked miracles in the centuries since Biblical times. Patterns of civilization have been greatly altered by new inventions and technological developments. It is difficult to judge the application of Biblical passages by reference to a world so completely different from the current situation. Yet this task must be undertaken if there is to be any genuine understanding of drinking in Bible times.

It has already been implied in the discussion of the meanings of the Hebrew and Greek words for wine that fermentation of all fruit juices was the normal expectation. Refrigeration was unknown in Palestine. No method was known by which fruit juice could be prevented from fermenting. Preservation of food was difficult. Often the food supply was small. Wine had a proper place as a food and a drink not needing refrigeration. Wine could be easily preserved.

Modern science has also made sanitation possible. Numerous regulations in the Bible and in the rabbinical teachings were measures requiring sanitary practices. Despite the best efforts of the ancient peoples, effective sanitation was impossible in many situations. Regulations governing the use of milk sought to eliminate illness due to the consumption of spoiled milk. It was both a food and a beverage, but its use could be dangerous.

The ancients had difficulties in obtaining proper beverages. Water was often unsafe. Effective filtration and chemical treatment of water are inventions of modern times. In many parts of the Old World the water supply is not hygienic even now. The use of untreated water as a beverage can spread disease germs and menace the health of a community.

The fermented fruit juice was a beverage free from germs. The alcohol in the wine made it a beverage uncontaminated by disease germs. It may well have been this property of wine which lay back of the advice to Timothy to "use a little wine for the sake of your stomach" (I Timothy 5:23). Wine was recognized in Biblical times as a drink which was dangerous when used immoderately. Although free from germs, the wine did have the possibility of harmful physical and mental effects. Although only a fermented beverage, wine was still capable of producing intoxication.

The alcoholic content of the wine mentioned in the Bible did not exceed 14 to 15 per cent. Fortified wines were unknown because the process of distillation was unknown. Such modern day wines as muscatel are fortified and have an alcoholic content of 20 per cent or more. It is doubtful that much of the Biblical wine was as strong even as 14 per cent alcohol. Probably only the wealthy had enough wine to allow the full fermentation process to occur. Drunkenness is most often referred to in the Scriptures as a sin of the rich. It is even likely that the wine of the common man was only mildly alcoholic.

DRUNKENNESS IN THE BIBLE

The low alcoholic content of the Biblical wine probably prevented drunkenness from becoming common. It is unlikely that there was an adequate supply of wine to make possible many drunken bouts for the person of average financial resources. Drunkenness required the consumption of a sizable amount of wine*. An average man of approximately 150 pounds weight would need to drink about one quart of wine without food to reach an alcoholic blood content of 0.15 per cent—the standard used in the uniform motor vehicle law to indicate intoxication. The consumption of nearly two quarts of fermented wine would be required to produce a drunken stupor. To produce these effects the wine must be consumed quickly because the normal bodily processes of oxidation and elimination work constantly. A person could drink about four ounces of wine per hour without increasing the alcohol content of his blood since regular bodily processes could remove that much alcohol.

It is unlikely that anyone in Biblical times became intoxicated by accident. Some traditions hold that Noah became drunk unawares due to changes in climatic conditions which made fermentation possible only after the Flood. These traditions rest only upon conjectures. Noah must have engaged in a long drinking bout to produce the stupor described.

Drunkenness is condemned throughout the Bible because anyone who became intoxicated had willed intoxication. He did not become drunk except as he drank large amounts over a long period. He could not become drunk while using wine as a food, for other foods eaten at the same time would slow the effects of alcohol consumption and would diminish the amount of alcohol which could be consumed. He could not become

*Throughout this paragraph the wine referred to is fermented wine—not fortified as are many wines used today.

drunk while using alcohol in ritual observances, for the rites did not cover an extended period of time. He was likely to become drunk only as he drank with riotous companions who had forgotten the Lord.

As the knowledge and use of the process of distillation became common, distilled spirits of high alcoholic content became available. The use of distilled spirits was capable of producing drunkenness quicker and with less consumption of alcohol. Accidental intoxication or unintentional intoxication became possible. Distilled spirits were cheaper in terms of absolute alcoholic content than were fermented beverages. Persons of limited financial resources could obtain enough spirits to become intoxicated.

Alcoholism could have developed in Biblical times from the use of fermented beverages, but it is impossible to determine from the records if any alcoholics existed. If any alcoholism prevailed prior to the discovery of distilled spirits, the incidence would certainly have been very small. The many pressures of the Jewish culture against drunkenness would operate against conditions giving rise to the development of alcoholism.

NEW DIMENSIONS OF THE PROBLEM

The use of distillation to produce beverages of high alcohol content added a new dimension to the Biblical picture of the use of wine. In the previous century many churchmen condemned the use of distilled spirits, but allowed the use of wines and beers. The use of wine in a world that had no distilled spirits—as in Biblical times—is quite different from the use of wine in a world in which distilled spirits are readily available. In Biblical times the only alcoholic drinks available were the so-called "beverages of moderation." Today nearly all drinkers begin their use of alcoholic beverages with the "beverages of moderation." A great majority of these drinkers then proceed to the use of distilled spirits. The use of beer and wine cannot be separated in our society from their effect upon the consumption of distilled spirits.

Furthermore, in our day distillation is highly commercialized. Some commerce in wine occurred in the ancient world, but the production of wine was largely a part of an agricultural economy. The family produced wine for its own use. The advent of distillation did not change this pattern rapidly. In colonial America many frontier farms had stills for the production of whiskey for the family. Thomas Jefferson stated that he hoped the government would never prohibit the farmer from having a still for the production of whiskey for his family. Frontiersmen often drank heavily, but not because of the urging of advertisements of distillers.

The alcohol industry is an important force in our society. It creates many pressures to stimulate the appetite to drink. Lobbyists exert pressure in legislatures. Economic pressures of many types operate to increase the use of alcohol. The alcohol industry is described in terms of the men employed and the dollars spent for agricultural products as well as the dollars spent for taxes. During the Depression of the early 1930's the alcohol industry claimed that the legalization of the sale of alcohol would bring back prosperity. Wealthy persons were assured that the legal sale of alcohol would produce enough revenues to allow reductions in the federal income tax.[3] Now the farmer is assured that the alcohol industry furnishes him a ready market for the grains which are flooding the normal food markets of the world. The support of labor unions is sought because of the jobs offered and the excellent labor record of the industry.

The alcohol industry has no hesitancy any more in advertising to create a demand for the use of wines, beers, and liquors. It assured the public in the early 1930's that a legalized alcohol industry would refrain from advertising. Now the industry claims the right to advertise since it is a legal, licensed business.

---

[3] Tun Yuan Hu, *The Liquor Tax in the United States, 1791-1947*, New York: Graduate School of Business, Columbia University, 1950, pp. 61-63.

Obviously the industry intends to use every economic pressure available to increase the consumption of alcohol. Motivational research is now being used in connection with advertising in order to use "hidden persuasion" to sell alcohol. Neither Jesus nor Paul ever had to contend with drinking practices influenced by such an industry.

A part of the alcohol industry is the retail outlet such as the bar or tavern. In such business establishments drinking is not primarily a family venture. In Biblical times drinking occurred within the family circle. One condemnation of drunkenness was leveled at the drinking with evil companions. It is not necessarily true that people in taverns and bars are looking for evil companions, but these are not the centers usually associated with family drinking. Dimly lit bars invite illegal and immoral liaisons which threaten the stability of the family.

Mechanization is another important factor in modern society unknown in Biblical times. In a mechanized society the loss of skill and efficiency due to the anesthetizing effect of alcohol is far more serious than in earlier times. Split-second precision is often needed for the operation of the machines commonly used in our society. Nowhere is the need for speedy, sure reactions more important than in the operation of motor vehicles. The high-speed automobile has greatly changed the seriousness of the alcohol problem within the last thirty years. The machine-age culture has added another new dimension to the whole question of the use of alcohol, even the moderate use of alcohol.

The increasing urbanization of modern society with the creation and expansion of great city areas is different from anything existing in Palestine in Biblical times. The cities of the ancient world were not comparable with the modern centers of population. It is in these great cities that the heaviest drinking now occurs. The tensions of urban life and the depersonalizing effects of modern assembly-line industry produce individuals more susceptible to immoderate drinking patterns.

In these great cities individuals can be unnoticed and unknown while in the midst of throngs. Many major cities have skid rows or areas of homeless men. Here gather those who have been defeated by the pressures and tensions of our culture. Alcohol is the constant companion of the homeless man. He is variously called bum, hobo, panhandler, or chronic police-case inebriate. He is not always an alcoholic, but he is nearly always intoxicated.

SCRIPTURAL INSIGHTS

In a slower, less technological, more stable culture such as prevailed in the New Testament era, drinking of wine in the absence of distilled liquors would not present as great problems as are presented today. It is our duty to search the Scriptures for their central meaning and their guidance for a day such as ours. We are not called upon to duplicate the patterns of Bible times. Rather we are to let the gospel speak to us so that redemption may work in our society.

Each man as he searches the Scriptures finds passages which seem pertinent to his daily routine. From various parts of the Bible different ones may hear statements that help define actions consistent with love of God, love of neighbor, and respect for oneself as the creature of God. Any course of action adopted must be regarded in terms of the response of Christian love.

Many Christians have found in Romans 14 an important statement relating to the duty of the Christian to his brother: "Then let us no more pass judgment on one another, but rather decide never to put a stumbling-block or hindrance in the way of a brother. I know and am persuaded in the Lord Jesus that nothing is unclean in itself; but it is unclean for any one who thinks it unclean. If your brother is being injured by what you eat, you are no longer walking in love. . . . Do not, for the sake of food, destroy the work of God. Everything is indeed clean, but it is wrong for any one to make others fall by what he eats; it is right not to eat meat or drink wine or do anything that makes your brother stumble" (13-15; 20-21).

In this passage Paul lays no commandments upon the Christians, but he advises as to the response of love to a weak brother. Evidently there were some Christians who had very sensitive consciences. They not only refused to eat meat or drink wine offered to idols, but refused to eat any meat or drink any wine. Indeed they seemed to be following another word of Paul in which he had said, "Abstain from every form of evil" (I Thessalonians 5:22). Although Paul did not agree with their self-denial, he did respect their consciences. From this regard for others he advised against any act which might offend.

It would be impossible to enact this principle into laws or rules. This principle does not deal with one's intention to offend. It proceeds rather from deep sensitivity to the weaknesses of our brothers. This zealous consideration of others and their well-being is stifled by any set of laws and rules. It lives and flourishes only as we seek to practice the Golden Rule. It calls for a depth of interpersonal relations and understanding that make the sacrificial act seem no sacrifice at all.

Some have tried to use this passage from Paul as the basis of rules for abstinence from drinking. One may well abstain from using alcohol as a fulfillment of this Scripture, but the full meaning is not so easily fulfilled. The abstainer should also be willing to forego other rights and privileges for the salvation of his brother. Abstinence for the sake of the weak brother who may be a potential alcoholic is only one step in the process of understanding and alleviating the weakness.* The response of Christian love includes much more.

Advocates of moderate drinking all too often insist upon their rights. The law defines and guarantees rights. Paul has not removed the rights of anyone to drink or eat meat. He has instead called attention to the dimensions of love. An insistence upon one's rights without consideration of the brother's weakness is a denial of love. The weak brother has no rights which

---

* The teaching of Paul reflects the spirit of the Sermon on the Mount and the more emphatic saying of Jesus in Matthew 18:6-9.

demand abstinence from the strong brother. The response of love is the disciplined denial of one's rights lest the weakness of the brother bring destruction. No Christian can disregard his brother's weaknesses, no matter how foolish or absurd it is.

In the midst of a society such as ours, compulsive drinking is widespread. The compulsive drinker is our brother. Christians must respond in love to this weakness. The surrender of any right to drink moderately on behalf of the weak brother who is incapable of drinking moderately seems a proper Christian response to the needs of the brother.

Every Christian is reminded that he is a creature of God. Paul called it to the attention of the Corinthians in these words: "Do you not know that your bodies are members of Christ? . . . Do you not know that your body is a temple of the Holy Spirit . . . ?" (I Corinthians 6:15, 19.) These questions indicate that every Christian must regard himself in terms of his relation to God. This leaves no room for self-centeredness. Even as one looks at himself he must see his relation to God as paramount. He is called to a stewardship of his body. It is God's creation and is to be held in trust for him.

Anything which lessens the abilities of the body or detracts from continuous recognition of one's relation to God is a violation of the stewardship of the body. For many, alcohol does have demonstrable effects as a central nervous system depressant, of temporarily removing physical skills and judgmental talents. Alcohol is therefore renounced in line with the understanding of stewardship.

There are no simple Biblical rules that will spell out how one's stewardship is to be discharged. Rather, in the Bible one finds a revelation of God and his ways with men. Ethical decisions stem from the revelation of God and his love for man. The struggle to ascertain one's rights is lost in the word: "Greater love has no man than this, that he will lay down his life for a friend."

CHAPTER V

Alcohol and the Churches

THE early Christian Church followed rather closely the ethic of Judaism. The New Testament writings served for the ethical guide once the process of canonization was complete in the second century. Only rarely did the early Church feel the necessity of adopting new ethical standards for the conduct of its members.

THE EARLY CHURCH

The early Christians did not practice abstinence as far as we are able to learn. Doubtless some individual Christians did follow a practice of drinking no wine, but their numbers were not great nor was their influence important. A reference by Clement of Alexandria praises those Christians who have adopted an austere way of life in that they drink water instead of wine. Clement himself cried out against drunkenness but allowed that the moderate use of wine made the heart to rejoice. The prevailing ethic of the Church declaimed against insobriety and permitted moderate drinking of wine.

Only ascetic heresies demanded abstinence as part of the Christian ethic. Under Greek influence several Christian heresies arose which declared that the world and the flesh were evil while only the spirit was good. These heresies usually demanded that Christians suppress physical appetites to the greatest extent possible. The Gnostics constituted the leading ascetic heresy. Some of them renounced wine, war, and women. Water was substituted for wine in the Holy Communion.

Some orthodox Christians in North Africa also substituted water for wine in the Eucharist, but for an entirely different reason. During a period of persecution they feared that the odor of wine could be detected on the breath after early morning mass. Fearing detection as Christians, they made a pragmatic substitution, but without any condemnation of the use of wine as a beverage. The drinking of wine later in the day would not arouse any suspicions that they were Christians. This substitutionary practice was short-lived.

Problems relating to the use of wine faced the Church in North Africa. They arose from the unwillingness of pagans to give up intemperance. St. Augustine felt that the Church relaxed its standard too frequently in order that it might get the pagans to accept Christianity. He labored hard to stamp out drunkenness in his diocese in North Africa, but he did not advocate abstinence. Rather, he declared wine to be the gift of God, but this declaration stemmed from his attacks upon another group of ascetic heretics, the Manichaeans.

MONASTICISM

Some monastic orders did follow a practice of abstinence. The monastic despaired of establishing any Christian society upon earth. He retired to a monastic center and renounced various fleshly pleasures. Celibacy, fasting, and abstinence were common. Pachomius, Columban of Ireland, and Boniface all established monasteries in which abstinence was required.

Not all monasteries forbade the use of wine. In fact, many of the more famous orders allowed the use of alcoholic beverages. St. Benedict established a monastic order which became famous for production of an alcoholic beverage.

St. Jerome and St. Augustine both praised abstinence. Each of them regarded abstinence as indicative of seriousness of purpose in the pursuit of holiness. Both associate abstinence with vegetarianism. Jerome remarked: "If you wish to be perfect, it is good not to drink wine and eat flesh." Augustine noted that saints perpetually abstained from the use of meat and wine.

The monks who practiced abstinence did so in the belief that a higher holiness was expected of men in the orders than of laymen. There was no expectation that laymen would practice abstinence or celibacy. The ascetic rules were all tied in to a dual standard of morality.

THE MIDDLE AGES

During the Middle Ages the problems of alcohol changed little. At festivals, including church festivals, many celebrants became intoxicated. The pulpits continued to rail against drunkenness. Occasional drunkenness was denounced as a venial sin while habitual drunkenness was damned as a mortal sin. Preachers used various techniques to halt the swelling tide of intoxication: satire, ridicule, and church plays. The secular world responded in kind, ridiculing drunken priests.

During the Middle Ages various rulers, either in their own name or in the name of the church, established laws governing the sale and use of alcoholic beverages. No one of them passed a law forbidding the use of alcohol; they only sought to regulate its use in the interests of sobriety. The control of the sale and use of alcohol traces back to Catholic Europe in the Middle Ages.

THE PROTESTANT REFORMATION

The early Protestants did not differ greatly from the Roman Catholic Church in their approach to alcohol. All the Reformers of renown used wine or beer.

Martin Luther was scathing in his denunciation of drunkenness. He knew that men sometimes grew merry with drink, but this seemed hardly worth criticism. He was greatly disturbed and scandalized at the drinking practices of many Christians who became soused. He refused to acknowledge that these drinkers were men, but held that they were swine.

Luther's personal drinking has been the subject of numerous anecdotes. Luther did enjoy eating and drinking, but apparently did not become intoxicated—even occasionally. Under stress Luther went for several days without food or beer.

Luther did not hesitate to speak out against violations of temperance. Even his own prince did not escape his sermons. One of his harshest statements was directed against the brewing industry: "The man who first brewed beer was a pest for Germany. Food must be dear in all our land, for the horses eat up all our oats, and the peasants drink up all our barley in the form of beer. I have survived the end of genuine beer, for it has now become small beer in every sense; and I have prayed to God that he might destroy the whole beer-brewing business; and the first beer-brewer I have often cursed. There is enough barley destroyed in the breweries to feed all Germany." [1]

John Calvin was no practicer of abstinence either, but he was less given to drinking than Luther. There is recorded that he accepted a gift of a cask of wine from the town council. He condemned drunkenness but did not speak against the moderate use of wine. The Calvinists did, however, institute a very strict discipline governing life as part of the Christian ethic. Dancing, card playing, gambling, obscenity, and drunkenness were opposed to the upright life. All the elect (the true Christians) would live the upright life. Christianity had not known previously any more rigorous approach to ethics than was established by the followers of John Calvin.

Calvin believed that the holy commonwealth could be set up on earth. He attempted to govern Geneva as if it were the city of God. He revived the medieval laws regulating the sale of alcohol, but soon adopted more rigorous regulations. Taverns were abolished and replaced by hostels. No person showing the slightest signs of being affected by alcohol was allowed to purchase drinks. No drinks were served after 9 p.m., and the drinkers were required to leave the dining room at that hour.

John Knox, in his religious leadership of Scotland, did not

---

[1] Quoted in Everett Tilson, *Should Christians Drink?* Nashville: Abingdon Press, 1957, p. 48.

differ much from Calvin. The Scotch reformer had his wine cellar. Knox opposed the "Book of Lawful Sports" which King James had sponsored. This book listed sports legal for the Sabbath in an attempt to prevent drunkenness and rowdy drinking. Knox defied the king on the issue of Sabbath desecration, although he was also opposed to drunkenness and intemperance.

The Anabaptists of Germany were the first Protestants requiring abstinence. These Anabaptists were the first sectarians among the new reformers. They held many beliefs quite similar to the Calvinists' but insisted upon even greater severity in ethics. The Anabaptists thought that the Lutherans had not insisted upon ethical purity as true reformers should.

The Anabaptists did not allow members to be public innkeepers or to sell any alcoholic beverage. They held that the sure path to sobriety is abstinence. The Lutheran Formula of Concord listed the prohibition against innkeeping as one of the errors of the Anabaptists. These sectarians were bitterly opposed on many grounds by both Lutherans and Calvinists. The attacks against them do not, however, do discredit to the Anabaptists.

A Lutheran minister in 1531 stated that a Christian could defend himself against charges of Anabaptist heresy by engaging in frequent drinking bouts. All too many Christians were willing to comply with this advice. It was indeed a strange situation when the intoxication of a man could be used to prove his orthodox Christianity, while sobriety could be used to serve as the basis of a charge of heresy. The Anabaptists were suppressed in Germany. They were either killed, converted, or forced to migrate to another country. The religious migrants had great influence in England upon the Quakers and Non-Conformists. In the United States their descendants include the various branches of the Church of the Brethren (Dunkards, Amish, Mennonites).

German Pietism, which arose at a later date, turned back to the Anabaptists for inspiration. Although not lineal descendants

91

of the Anabaptists, they were deeply affected by the ethical rigorism of the early sectarians. The German Pietists in turn had great influence upon John Wesley during the period when he was searching for a satisfactory religious experience. The Methodists adopted much of the ethical rigorism of the Anabaptists.

CHURCHES IN COLONIAL AMERICA

In colonial America there were no churches that advocated abstinence. In Georgia Oglethorpe attempted to prevent the use of any distilled liquors, but his efforts were not marked by much success. This effort at legal control of the use of alcohol was largely philanthropic rather than doctrinal.

In all other colonies it was the common opinion that alcoholic beverages were both beneficial and necessary. It was also the common practice to rebuke any excessive use of alcohol. The intoxicated were charged with violating God's will by abusing one of nature's wholesome gifts. The liquor problem consisted of the failure of individuals to exercise self-control. As early as 1622, however, we find that colonial authorities were concerned about widespread drunkenness.

The American Indian confronted the early colonists with a serious problem arising from excessive drinking. The Indians had no drinking habits derived from their culture, for alcohol had been unknown. When introduced to whiskey by the white man, the Indians rapidly acquired habits of drunkenness. A temperate Indian was soon quite rare. Under the influence of alcohol many Indians became marauders. So, although the colonists allowed the use of alcohol by all white men, laws were early written on the books forbidding the sale or gift of alcohol to any Indian.

The laws against the liquor trade with the Indians were enforced in every colony. Serious attempts were made to stamp out the traffic. In Connecticut some culprits were flogged for the offence of supplying liquor to the Indians. Some of the leading citizens of New Netherlands were deported back to Holland for engaging in the illegal trade. The laws were gradually modified because of economic pressures. In commenting upon the changes, Krout observed: "Everywhere the profits of commercial intercourse tended to break down the safeguards which the legislators threw about the traffic." [2] The desire for financial gain became more important than the protection of the Indian from insobriety.

Intoxicants could not be sold legally to Negroes, servants, or apprentices. The alcohol business was controlled by law under special licenses and regulations in every colony from the very beginning. Restrictions were imposed with the primary purpose of the prevention of intoxication or habitual tippling. Some laws granted preferential treatment to innkeepers, brewers, and distillers. These enterprises were encouraged; for the alcohol business was already looked upon as a source of tax revenue. They were also encouraged in order that imports of alcohol from Europe could be reduced. Brewers and vintners were particularly encouraged in order that beverages of low alcoholic content would be available to replace the heavy consumption of liquor.

In 1727 the revenue from the rum tax was given to Yale for the "use, benefit, and better support of the said college, its rectors and tutors." [3] At Harvard in 1653 the son of a tavernkeeper was listed as occupying the highest social position of any graduate of that year. In New England communities the most prominent citizen was encouraged to open a tavern. It was deemed important that only the most responsible citizens should be entrusted with the right to sell alcohol. The social position of the taverner could be lowered by the injudicious sale of alcohol. The sale of liquor was under the dual controls of law and social pressure. By the eighteenth century the occupation had suffered a great decline in status. Many persons of ques-

---

[2] John Allen Krout, *The Origins of Prohibition*, New York: Alfred A. Knopf, 1925, p. 5.
[3] Quoted in *ibid.*, p. 19.

tionable reputation were able to secure licenses for the sale of alcohol.

There were among the Puritans those who early found fault with the common practices regarding alcohol. Cotton Mather, noted preacher, accused his fellow citizens of deliberately intoxicating the Indians. He was joined in his denunciations by Increase Mather, who called for the banishment of all habitual drunkards. He claimed that certain illnesses were sent upon the intemperate by God's displeasure. Governor Bradford reproved Increase Mather because his sermons against alcohol became quite personal, but the sermons continued. Following the lead of these two eminent ministers, sermons against drunkenness were preached from many New England pulpits.

"Intemperance, resulting from flagrant abuse of nature's gifts, conflicted with Calvinistic ideas of frugality and respectability, which had it that liquor was given to man for the benefit of the group and not for the wasteful gratification of individual appetites. Therefore, by moral precept and statutory provision, the ban was placed upon drunkenness. He who stepped over the shadowy line of moderation, was an outcast from the community. His pathway was in side streets and back alleys, lest his presence offend his more sober fellows. Summary punishment was his lot if he dared to parade his offence on the public highway." [4]

Despite the efforts of the Puritan clergy, drunkenness increased. In the early eighteenth century the colonial habit of temperate drinking had almost vanished. The availability and popularity of rum worked changes in drinking customs. Horatio Sharpe, governor of Maryland, declared that the consumption of rum had become a disgrace to the colony. He found it necessary to condemn the morals of certain clergy who were habitual drunkards.

By the middle of the eighteenth century drunkenness had become a major problem in the colonies. Various churches

---

[4] *Ibid.*, p. 27.

sensed their responsibility to change this condition. More attention was directed to declaiming against intemperance and to praising sobriety as a virtue. The Quakers furnished the most effective and consistent opposition to the increasing use of alcoholic beverages. Some societies disciplined members for intemperance. Other societies sought to prevent the sale of spirituous liquors. The Yearly Meeting in 1736 and thereafter warned members against frequent use of alcoholic beverages. The Society of Friends had not yet become committed to total abstinence, but it was moving toward stringent rules against the misuse of alcohol. Near the end of the century some societies moved to force their members out of the liquor business.

EARLY METHODISTS

The Quakers and the Methodists were the first leaders in organized temperance crusades. They were soon joined by other religious groups, but to these two sects does the movement owe its beginning.

The Methodist movement did not begin until habits of drunkenness were well established, both in this country and in Britain. The early Methodists were moved by the many evils attendant upon the use of alcohol. The distillation of cheap gin in Britain made possible a widespread use of spirituous liquors. Prior to the production of this cheap liquor economic factors prevented the poorer people from frequent intoxication. An official government report of 1735-36 called attention to the many social evils arising from the great increase in the use of gin. Whole families were reported as being drunken simultaneously.

JOHN WESLEY

Wesley and the early Methodist leaders had a great ministry to the lower economic classes. These early Methodists were able to see at first hand the hardships brought about by drink. The many arguments used by the early Methodists against the use of alcohol are as frequently sociological as theological. The control of the use of liquor was looked upon as a first step in the righting of many evils plaguing society.

Wesley did not at first see the necessity of total abstinence. He and others of the reformers required abstinence from the use of distilled beverages and moderation in the use of beer, ale, and wine. He became convinced, however, that the reformed drinker could not use these fermented drinks without lapsing back into his old intemperate patterns. Moderate drinkers were urged to stop drinking for the sake of the weaker brother:

"You see the wine when it sparkles in the cup, and are going to drink it; I tell you there is poison in it, and therefore beg you to throw it away! You answer, the wine is harmless in itself. I reply, perhaps it is so; but still, if it be mixed with what is not harmless, no one in his senses, if he knows it, at least unless he could separate the good from the evil, will once think of drinking it. If you add, it is not poison to me, though it may be to others; then I say, throw it away for thy brother's sake, lest thou embolden him to drink also. Why should thy strength occasion thy weak brother to perish, for whom Christ died? Now, let anyone judge which is the charitable person, he who pleads against the wine for his brother's sake, or he who pleads against the life of his brother for the sake of wine?" [5]

Wesley was far more opposed to the liquor industry than to the individual user of alcohol. He reckoned the industry as unconcerned about the welfare of humanity, while the drinker was looked upon as weak in will. In his famous sermon on "The Use of Money" Wesley declared:

"Neither may we gain by hurting our neighbor in his body, therefore we may not sell anything which tends to impair

[5] *Arminian Magazine*, Vol. XX, 1797, p. 487.

health. Such is eminently all that liquid fire, commonly called drams, or spirituous liquors. . . . All who sell them in the common way, to any that will buy, are poisoners general. They murder His Majesty's subjects by wholesale, neither does their eye pity nor spare. They drive them to hell like sheep: and what is their gain? Is it not the blood of these men? Who, then, would envy their estates and sumptuous palaces? A curse is in the midst of them. Blood, blood is there: the foundation, the floor, the walls, the roof, are stained with blood."

THE WESLEYAN RULE

The rules of the Methodist societies in 1743 required members to avoid "drunkenness, buying or selling spirituous liquors, or drinking them, unless in cases of extreme necessity." These General Rules are still a part of the *Doctrines and Discipline of The Methodist Church*. This injunction against the use of hard liquors was made the basis of dismissal of many members from the early societies. Wesley did not think alcohol was of much value as a medicine, but he did allow its use when deemed necessary by a physician. He observed in his sermon on "The Use of Money": "It is true, these [spirituous liquors] may have a place in medicine (although there would be rarely any occasion for them, were it not for the unskilfulness of the practitioner)."

Wesley included in his crusade against alcohol a condemnation of the too common use of alcohol as a medicine. In 1756 he wrote in the *Arminian Magazine* that spirituous liquors caused many diseases—more than it could cure. He advised that *small* beer could perform all the functions of medication necessary.[6] Water was praised as the most wholesome of drinks while malt liquors "except clear *small* beer or ale" were capable of producing great hurt.

Wesley did use appeals to economic factors as important rea-

[6] *The Works of the Rev. John Wesley,* London, 1809, Vol. XII, p. 299.

sons for his opposition to alcoholic beverages. In 1773 and 1778 he attributed the scarcity of food to the use of large quantities of grain in distilling. (This argument is reminiscent of Luther's attack upon the brewers of Germany.)

The Methodist Church in the United States acknowledged the leadership of Wesley. In the rules for the American Conference of 1780 Wesley required the ministers to disapprove of distillation of hard liquors. Also, ministers were required to disown all friends who would not give up the practice of distilling liquor. Some Methodists in America did not agree wholeheartedly with Wesley's position, but more stringent rules were adopted by the Conferences until the Methodist Church was firmly committed to an obligatory practice of total abstinence.

In 1747 Wesley wrote the Bishop of London acknowledging that total abstinence was not absolutely required of all Christians.[7] He did mention in the letter that he had already abstained for about ten years and that he had no intention of ever drinking any alcohol again. This resolve was fulfilled and later used by Wesley to explain his good health and longevity.

Wesley found it hard to understand how any serious Christian could use *any* alcoholic beverage in the midst of widespread drunkenness. Because of the greater drunkenness in Ireland he stated that in that country, above all others, the duty to abstain was greatest.[8] His principle of total abstinence, followed by Methodists here, derives in large measure from the need for radical measures to solve the tremendous problem of drunkenness.

THE TEMPERANCE MOVEMENT

The early Methodists found that Quakers were hard at work in fighting against intemperance. The most influential worker for temperance in the late eighteenth century was a Quaker physician, Benjamin Rush. Dr. Rush, a signer of the Declara-

---

[7] *Ibid.*, Vol. VIII, p. 489.
[8] *Ibid.*, Vol. VIII, p. 232.

tion of Independence and a renowned statesman, became greatly disturbed by the drunkenness of many soldiers in the Continental Army. In 1778 he published a tract in which he stated that spirituous liquors did not relieve fatigue, sustain hard labor, nor protect against cold and heat. He was sure that the usual ration of rum given to the soldier prevented him from being as effective in waging war as his potential.

In 1784, Dr. Rush published a pamphlet, *An Inquiry into the Effects of Spirituous Liquors on the Human Body and Mind*. As a medical man of great reputation he cited numerous cases of disease and mental illness which he traced to the use of alcohol. He even reasoned that the long-term use of spirits, even in moderation, would result in serious physical and mental health problems. This booklet was widely distributed and had a great effect in arousing opposition to the use of alcohol. At harvest time each year the pamphlet was sent to farmers in an attempt to stop the practice of furnishing liquor as a part of the day's wages. By 1850 more than 200,000 copies of Rush's pamphlet had been distributed.

The temperance movement quickly spread following this important work of Rush. In Connecticut farmers banded together in an agreement that only beer or cider would be furnished as alcoholic drinks to their workmen. At Yale President Timothy Dwight tried to persuade the students to give up drinking. He held that the road to drunkenness began with moderate drinking. Jonathan Edwards adopted abstinence as the principle of his life, although he made no such request of others. His sermons occasionally extolled the benefits which he had received from abstinence.

Another powerful figure in the temperance movement was Lyman Beecher. Beecher was reared in a home in which liquor was never served—a practice in sharp contrast with the behavior of his neighbors. As a student at Yale he had agreed with the temperance sermons of President Dwight. He had sharply opposed the habits of many of the students who coupled profanity, gambling, and licentiousness with their drunkenness. From this preparation came one of America's greatest and most influential preachers. His memory is still perpetuated in the great Lyman Beecher Lectureship at Yale.

Timothy Dwight and Lyman Beecher attacked temperate drinking as the prelude to intemperate drinking. From their leadership a new phase of the temperance movement developed. Beecher traced his opposition to temperate drinking to a boisterous scene following his ordination. All the ministers drank, and many were hilarious and foolish in their conduct. This misconduct on the part of ministers at a solemn occasion aroused Beecher to fighting pitch.

Using his pulpit at Litchfield, Connecticut, as a rallying point, Beecher entered into politics and organized efforts to suppress vice as well as intemperance. Various church groups went on record as favoring the temperance movement. In 1812 the General Assembly of Presbyterians called on all preachers to advocate temperance and to preach against all habits and indulgences which might lead to intemperance.

The first permanent society for promoting temperance was formed in New York in 1808. In 1826 the most famous of the societies, the American Society for the Promotion of Temperance, was organized in Boston. In 1827 the General Assembly of the Presbyterian Church approved the work of the American Temperance Society. Soon Dutch Reformed, Methodist, Congregational, and Baptist bodies also endorsed the work of the temperance society. Lutherans and Episcopalians were railed upon by these denominations because of indifference to reform. These reactions were not altogether fair, as Bishops Otey and McIlvaine of the Episcopal Church supported the temperance movement.

The temperance societies were largely composed of active churchmen. The work of the temperance cause often resembled a revival meeting more than anything else. Some of the churches, however, were sharply critical of the temperance societies. A Dutch Reformed congregation in Breakabeen, New York, denounced the movement and forbade members to belong to a temperance society. Primitive Baptist churches in Tennessee expelled members who joined temperance societies.

The support received by the temperance societies from the churches resulted in tremendous growth and influence. In 1834 incomplete statistics indicated that there were more than 5,000 local branches of the American Temperance Society and that these groups had more than a million members. In that year the New York society reported that more than 130 distilleries had gone out of business between 1829 and 1834.

During this first phase of the temperance movement the abstinence position was not obligatory. Believers in abstinence worked side by side with those who permitted the moderate use of fermented beverages. All temperance workers were opposed to the use of distilled spirits, even in moderation, because of the danger of intemperance posed by liquors. During this first phase there was little effort directed toward legislation to outlaw the liquor industry. Rather, the movement was a great cooperative crusade of a religious nature.

In 1836 the American Temperance body adopted a binding pledge for all members that they would work for "total abstinence from all that can intoxicate." This pledge resulted in a sharp decline in the numbers and the financial support of the organization. In the same year pressure was also begun to secure legislation prohibiting the manufacture and sale of all intoxicants. Four years later the body went on record in opposition to the use of wine in the Lord's Supper.

FROM THE MAINE LAW TO PROHIBITION

Although the temperance movement declined greatly in size of membership following the split over the issue of total abstinence, it continued influential. By 1851 it had been most instrumental in securing the passage of a model prohibition law in Maine. This Maine Liquor Law was widely copied. By 1855 a total of 13 states and territories had adopted laws making the sale and distribution of liquor illegal. A reaction against these laws occurred in the wake of the Civil War. By 1870 only two states still retained their laws against liquor.

In 1874 the women of the churches organized into a militant temperance group. This National Woman's Christian Temperance Union continues in existence to the present day. In fact, it now has substantially more members than it had a decade ago. The W. C. T. U. carried on a program quite similar to the earlier temperance movements. It too was closely related to the churches. Without question it was one of the most important agencies for the cause of nationwide legislation.

The women also went into saloons, seeking to persuade the vendors to give up the business. In some cases the appeals met with success. The women pictured their crusade as an effort to protect the innocent from the abuses connected with the use of alcohol.

The Prohibition Party was formed in 1872 with the primary aim of the securing of national prohibition. This party had other important goals also. It was essentially a liberal third-party movement, but its stand on the use of alcohol was not accepted by many liberals. Many of the early planks in the platform of the Prohibition Party were enacted into law under the administrations of Theodore Roosevelt and Franklin D. Roosevelt.* This political party was one in which many ministers and other churchmen labored long hours. No other political party has received so much support from official church bodies as did the Prohibition Party.

The Anti-Saloon League was another agency which worked for nationwide prohibition. This organization was not a political party, but it was a political organization. It used the tactics of political machines to secure the election of candidates

---

* These enactments were, of course, social and economic reforms, not the prohibition of alcohol.

advocating prohibition. It was effective in many instances, but its ethics and tactics were often subject to criticism.

By 1916 state-wide prohibition laws were in effect in 19 states. Local option laws were in effect in 26 other states, permitting localities to forbid the manufacture, transportation or sale of alcohol. Only three states had no provisions by which the sale of alcohol could be outlawed. In 1919 the Eighteenth Amendment was ratified. On January 16, 1920, it became the law of the land that the sale of beverage alcohol was forbidden.

THE WASHINGTONIANS

Not all of the forces working for abstinence had concerned themselves with legislation. In 1840 six reformed drunkards in Baltimore organized a society known as the Washingtonians. These alcoholics cooperated with each other in securing sobriety. They held closed meetings to discuss their problems. They had an auxiliary agency of wives and relatives known as the Martha Washingtons. Prominent persons were invited to speak to the groups. Many prominent persons enlisted in the movement in a desire to help the drunkard become sober. Over 600,-000 persons joined the movement. It is believed that at least 100,000 drunkards were returned to sobriety through this group and its program.

The Washingtonians were the first temperance workers to devote major efforts at rehabilitation. Some church people opposed the group because they thought that the testimonies were untruthful. Others resented the fact that many of the reformed drunkards did not immediately become active in churches. Many other churchmen including prominent leaders, however, did cooperate with the efforts of this early forerunner of Alcoholics Anonymous.

ROMAN CATHOLIC TEMPERANCE MOVEMENTS

About the same time that the Washingtonian movement was at its peak of influence Father Mathew was accomplishing great results in working with alcoholics in Ireland. This Roman Catholic priest sought pledges of abstinence from all Irish to whom he could speak. He believed that total abstinence was the best approach to the rehabilitation and prevention of chronic drunkenness. He did not preach this as a requirement of faith, but as a vow to be assumed for special purposes. In his labors in Ireland he secured more than 4,500,000 pledges of total abstinence. In securing this great number of pledges—perhaps more than the present population of Ireland—he effectively changed the country's whole social drinking pattern. From the time of Father Mathew to the present, alcoholism in Ireland has never assumed the proportions of the national calamity that existed in the 1840's.

Father Mathew came to the United States in 1849 and remained till 1851, working among the many Irish immigrants who had so recently come to the country. Although he did not achieve results as outstanding as in his Irish campaign, at least 156,000 pledges were signed. Some estimate that as many as 500,000 signed pledges of total abstinence.

In 1890 another total abstinence movement was organized within the Roman Catholic Church in the United States. The Catholic Union for Promoting Total Abstinence and the movement known as The Sacred Thirst received the blessing of Pope Leo XIII. Numerous priests and laymen became members of the movement and took pledges of total abstinence. They even sought to change the saloonkeepers. All who sold intoxicating liquor were urged to choose "a more honorable way of making a living." [9] If they continued to sell alcohol, they must not sell to the young nor those whom they could foresee would abuse drink.

---

[9] Quoted in Sister Joan Bland, *Hibernian Crusade: The Story of the Catholic Total Abstinence Union of America,* Washington: Catholic University of America Press, 1951, p. 127.

THE EIGHTEENTH AMENDMENT

These various movements working for temperance represented the opinions of the great majority of the American people. There was no trickery by which the Eighteenth Amendment was passed. In the 1880's various states passed laws requiring alcohol education in the public schools. These laws were soon in force in nearly all the states. Their influence helped the churches attack the evils of drink.

The Rockefeller Commission sponsored a famous study of liquor control. This study, published in 1933 at the end of the effectiveness of the Eighteenth Amendment, said: "It is scarcely an exaggeration to say that the liquor business, as organized before prohibition, stood for everything that decency was opposed to and fought everything that decency desired. That there were individuals here and there in both the retail and wholesale business who were respectable and socially responsible citizens must, of course, be admitted. But their voices were unheard in the clamor of the trade for increased profits. . . . In large measure the Eighteenth Amendment was the final result of angry public reaction, accumulative over a long period of years, against a system that debauched personal character, corrupted public life, and defied control." [10]

The results of the Eighteenth Amendment are still hotly debated more than a quarter century after the repeal of the amendment. There were numerous reasons that made a majority of the populace ready for an end to the "experiment noble in purpose." With the end of the complete banning of legal sales of liquors in Oklahoma in 1959, only one state is nominally "dry." Few citizens of Mississippi can claim that the state is successful in enforcing its laws which make the sale of liquor illegal.

The repeal of the Eighteenth Amendment forced the advocates of temperance within the churches to modify their pro-

[10] Raymond Fosdick and Albert Scott, *Toward Liquor Control*, New York: Harper and Brothers, 1933, p. 148.

grams. Some substantial modification of views also occurred. Many lost interest in the question of alcohol. Others pursued programs no more comprehensive than an occasional sermon or discussion on drunkenness.

MODERN CHURCHES SPEAK ON ALCOHOL

The Federal Council of Churches spent $150,000 on temperance activities in the period 1916-20. Neither the Federal Council nor the National Council has allocated comparable budgetary amounts to any type of temperance program in the period since 1920. The National Council of Churches had difficulties in devising temperance programs which would enlist the support of the member denominations. In 1958 the General Board of the National Council did issue a pronouncement which was supported by the constituent churches.

The pronouncement did not take any stand on the issue of abstinence versus the moderate use of alcohol. It did find important aspects of the problem upon which the churches could cooperate as they sought solutions to the problems of alcohol. Important items in the report stated:

"We recognize that the alcohol problem is related to other social problems. Thus, another means of social control involves the removal of degrading social conditions such as poverty, disease, bad housing, poor education, and inadequate recreational and health facilities. Effective social control involves strengthening family life and creating a wholesome moral atmosphere. It involves providing mental health clinics, family case work agencies, and pastoral counseling programs as a means of strengthening persons emotionally and socially. . . .

"The churches' efforts, properly directed to the achievement of adequate programs of education, Christian teaching, and social renewal will make more effective whatever legal controls may be necessary. The general public must be protected from those whose drinking endangers others. The legal controls relating to beverage alcohol should be aimed to reduce its use. .... There is wide agreement among the churches with regard to legal restraints on driving while under the influence of alcohol and on the sale of alcoholic beverages to minors."

Some Protestant bodies still hold abstinence unnecessary. These bodies work for moderation in drinking. The Protestant Episcopal Church has traditionally held such a position. Recently this denomination has evidenced great interest in alleviating the problems arising from the intemperate use of alcohol, but it has done this within the framework of its traditional position allowing moderate drinking.

American Churches That Urge Abstinence From the Use of Alcoholic Beverages*

American Baptist Convention
American Lutheran Church
Augustana Lutheran Church
Church of the Brethren
Church of the Nazarene
Disciples of Christ
The Five Years Meeting of Friends
Free Methodist Church of North America
The Methodist Church
Moravian Church of America, North and South

Presbyterian Church in the United States
United Presbyterian Church in the USA
Reformed Church in America
Reformed Presbyterian Church of North America
Seventh-Day Adventists
Southern Baptist Convention
United Church of Christ
United Lutheran Church in America

---

* From a pamphlet of the Board of Temperance of The Methodist Church

A Joint Commission on Alcoholism of the Protestant Episcopal Church published a report which has been given wide publicity. This report is not an official action of the Church. The report does recognize the right of any Christian to follow a program of total abstinence, but abstainers are pictured by implication as self-righteous prudes. Some of the most constructive thinking in the report is included in the section on the responsibility of a host or hostess. There are pertinent items in this report which many church members (Episcopal, Methodist and others) need to observe:

"1. Never give a party for the main or sole purpose of drinking. . . .

"4. If alcoholic drinks are served, serve always with them, and as attractively, non-alcoholic drinks.

"5. Never violate courtesy by allowing pressure to be put on guests to drink if they do not wish to do so.

"6. Never delegate to cocktails the host's responsibility to create an atmosphere, and to encourage relationships, conducive to wholesome recreation.

"7. Avoid drawing attention to a guest who is known to have the illness of alcoholism." [11]

The Episcopal Church is deeply interested in ministering to alcoholics. Although no statistics are available to support this conjecture, it appears that a greater proportion of Episcopal ministers are actively working with alcoholics than is true for any other denomination. The Joint Commission held up to the church its responsibility for ministry to alcoholics.

The Roman Catholic Church too is deeply concerned about the problems arising from the intemperate use of alcohol. Within the Roman church are many who abstain from the use of all alcoholic beverages for religious reasons. Within the United States, Canada, and Ireland there are organizations of Roman Catholics which advocate abstinence in the pursuit of holiness.

[11] *Alcohol, Alcoholism, and Social Drinking*, Greenwich, Connecticut: The Seabury Press, 1958, p. 26.

In Ireland 15 per cent of the people belong to the Pioneers, the total abstinence organization. Many young priests assume vows of abstinence during the first years following ordination. In numerous dioceses youth are urged to sign pledges to abstain from the use of alcoholic beverages until the age of twenty-one is reached.

In 1958 Roman Catholic children in the Spokane diocese were asked to sign a no-liquor pledge at the time of confirmation. One parent was asked to sign with each youngster. Bishop Bernard J. Topel announced the program and added: "Drinking is a very serious problem in our high schools, both Catholic and public. Some people think it is the greatest of all evils here. This is one way to cope with it." [12]

The Roman Catholic Church does not require abstinence of anyone, but rather recommends it. Sobriety is required and is a special virtue. Intemperate drinking is always condemned. The Roman Church is quite strict in its judgment of the results of irresponsible drinking.[13] The Roman Catholic Church is indeed serious in its program to combat the evils of beverage alcohol and has accomplished much that is praiseworthy.

The Reformed Church in America in an action of its General Synod in 1955 strongly urged the voluntary adoption of total abstinence by its members. The report of the Christian Action Commission was critical of all use of alcoholic beverages, even in moderate drinking.

The General Council of the Congregational Christian Churches, just before its union into a larger denomination, also strongly advocated the position of abstinence. It did not require abstinence, but it did indicate that the path of moderate drinking was so beset by pitfalls that any prudent Christian would choose the path of abstinence.

The Quakers have no official position on alcohol, but they continue in the long tradition of speaking against any use of

---

[12] *The Christian Century,* Vol. LXXV, No. 22, June 4, 1958, p. 673.
[13] See John C. Ford, *Man Takes a Drink,* New York: P. J. Kenedy & Sons, 1955.

alcohol. Abstinence is recommended as the superior way of showing one's responsibility for his brother.

The Church of the Brethren has been quite comprehensive in its concern about alcohol. It speaks with concern for the alcoholic, but recognizes that many discussions of alcoholism overlook the depth of the problem and the alcoholic's need of God. This church not only upholds abstinence, but advises its members to patronize businesses which do not sell alcohol. This latter position is not a boycott of those who sell alcohol, but is rather regarded as an attempt to relieve economic pressures upon the merchants who refuse to become a part of the liquor business.

The Seventh-Day Adventists, the Church of Christ, the Baptist bodies, and The Methodist Church all continue in their long-term positions of advocacy of total abstinence. Each of these bodies has consistently fought the alcohol interests on every front and in every situation conceivable. The Southern Baptist Convention and The Methodist Church are the two largest of these bodies, and, as such, they have adopted comprehensive programs relating to alcohol. Each of these two carries on a program directed toward education, rehabilitation, and social action of a variety of forms. These two denominations speak so often on the question of alcohol that no Christian denomination will ever be able to ignore the issues involved in the use of intoxicants.

CHAPTER VI

An Appeal to Christian Responsibility

THE use of alcohol as a beverage is responsible for many evils in our society. The Christian church and the Jewish synagogue have consistently opposed drunkenness. Other great religions in other parts of the world have also opposed intoxication. Obviously religion throughout the world is interested in helping man to find fulfillment without resorting to intoxication.

There is disagreement, however, as to the best method of removing evils arising from the use of alcoholic beverages. Within Christianity there are important differences in belief regarding alcohol. All branches of the Christian Church oppose drunkenness, but this is almost the only point of unity in their treatment of the alcohol question.

If the various churches cannot agree as to what is right relative to the use of alcohol, how then can individual Christians be sure in the way they handle alcohol? The question is an important one. In present-day society few choose their friends and associates from within the fellowship of one denomination. All are constantly brought into relationships with those who hold different views as to the proper attitude toward alcoholic beverages. If the differences are disregarded, the problems related to the use of alcohol seem to become unimportant.

DIFFERING CHRISTIAN DOCTRINES

There is a tendency to regard any definite statement about the use of alcohol as an expression of bigotry. An insistence that one's church is right may imply that the other's church is wrong. In the attempt to escape religious controversy, the use of beverage alcohol may fail of mention because of the variations in belief concerning it. An examination of the differences in belief may indicate in many instances that these differences arise from different methods used in determining the right. Christians do not use the same methods in arriving at their ethical systems.

Differences in belief concerning alcohol are related to other differences. Beliefs about alcohol are not the most important beliefs of any church. The control of alcohol needs to be viewed as one part of the larger issue of the good life. It is conceded by all churches that control of alcohol should never be emphasized to the point that it is considered as the complete fulfillment of Christian duty. Sobriety is just one of the virtues, and it stands in constant need of being complemented by the other virtues.

Some of the differences between churchmen relative to alcohol arise from the attention devoted to intoxication. Drunkenness is not the worst sin, nor are the problems arising from the use of alcohol the worst that prevail in our society. It does not contribute to understanding when alcohol is emphasized to the neglect of more important issues. The situation deserves the careful attention of Christians, particularly as they try to arrive at common understandings so that their cooperative efforts may make this a sober nation.

Some determine their ethical positions from reference to the Bible. All Christians refer to the Bible as they draw ethical conclusions, but not all rely upon the Bible as the sole ethical criterion. One denomination holds that it speaks when the Bible speaks and is silent when the Bible is silent.

Biblical views concerning the use of alcohol have already been discussed. A very brief statement of Biblical positions must include the consistent condemnation of intoxication and a record of the use of alcohol in moderation by certain good men. From such a brief summary some do draw their practices. Several denominations continue to point out that the Bible does not forbid the temperate use of alcohol. From this the conclusion is drawn that the temperate use of alcohol is allowed by the Christian faith.

Any serious attempt to use the Bible as a document specifically laying down abstinence rules proceeds from preconceived ethical rules. But the Bible does state truths and principles which may be related to a position of total abstinence.

A number of the churches which allow moderate drinking rely upon the Bible as the proof of the rightness of temperate drinking. If the church seeks to follow completely the pattern of Biblical times, it is justified in the moderate use of alcohol. But, it must be remembered, the Bible does not condemn slavery either. Slavery must be allowed too, then.

DIFFERING DENOMINATIONAL TRADITIONS

Others rely upon traditional views as they arrive at ethical decisions. The tradition includes the teachings and practices of the Christians deemed most significant in the development of the church. These may include the early Fathers of the church or they may refer only to more recent leaders. Since problems similar to the current ones have arisen in the past, the leaders of the past probably found solutions to similar issues. The wise answers of the great and good men are consulted for help in ethical dilemmas.

To varying degrees all churches rely upon tradition. The tradition of a modern sect may be limited indeed, but it is a vital force nevertheless. The tradition of many Methodists goes back no farther than John Wesley, while for others it goes back to the great Reformers. The Roman Catholics include the leaders of the early church, but so also do many Protestants.

The denominations with the longest histories tend to go back the farthest in the formation of their traditions. Previous discussion has indicated that during the greatest range of the history of the Christian church moderate drinking was consistently allowed. Such denominations, therefore, as the Roman Catholic, the Protestant Episcopal, and the Lutheran trace back in their tradition to a period when moderate drinking was universally approved.

The younger denominations have arisen since the process of distillation became well known. Methodism was born into a world in which drunkenness was a major evil because of the cheapness of gin. Quakers, Christian Scientists, and Baptists all have developed their traditions since drunkenness became widespread.

Reference to the Bible and to tradition can yield valuable insight into complex ethical problems. The addition of new dimensions to social problems, however, may make traditional and narrowly Biblical references of limited value. Every social problem needs to be viewed in terms of as many component parts as can be detected. Tradition and the Bible can speak to the ethical problems of our day, but interpretation in terms of modern-day life is necessary.

The denominations that support the abstinence position as the answer to the alcohol problem came into being as sects in revolt against the established churches. These sects decried the immorality present in the culture of their day. To escape the immorality they adopted a rigorous ethic. Many pleasures commonly allowed were condemned. Their ethical standards were exactly defined in order that there could be attained purity of life.

LEGALISTIC RELIGION

These complex systems of moral standards furnished the background for a new legalistic religion. This legalism emphasized the sins one must not engage in rather than the virtues that were the "fruit of the Spirit." The negative approach was apparent from the many admonitions that "thou shalt not."

By its very nature any legalistic religion develops self-righteous prudes. No matter how rigorous the code, some find deep satisfactions in fulfilling the most exacting demands of a legal religion. The achievement of the standard is productive of pride.

With pride the standard is rigidly maintained in order that not many others may achieve righteousness.

The whole emphasis in such legalistic systems is upon the achievement of man. Even when bitter denunciatory sermons are delivered against sinful men, the stress by implication is upon the success of certain good men. Emphases are placed upon the good works of which man is capable rather than upon the redeeming grace of God and the holiness which God's love produces in man. Salvation is pictured as being extended to those who are good.

There have been churchmen who followed a legalistic religion as they followed the practice of abstinence from the use of alcoholic beverages. These have talked long of the depraved condition of the drunkard. Those who tasted a drop of alcoholic beverages were consigned to the same status as the drunkard— they had fallen short of the legalistic ethic and its demand for perfect achievement. All use of alcohol was described in terms of the drunk in the gutter. Despite other patterns of drinking, all use of alcohol was condemned as productive of the worst excesses of the last-stage chronic alcoholic.

All too frequently these have defined the good life in terms of abstinence from alcohol and other vices. Some denominations questioned each applicant for membership as to his disposition toward these vices. A person could join certain churches only after a detailed statement of morality.

The Protestant Reformation was built upon the doctrine of justification by faith. It revolted against any system that conceived of salvation as deriving from good works. Jesus at the beginning of the Christian Era revolted against the self-righteousness of those who had gained goodness by holy works. Every Protestant today should still be in revolt against self-righteousness and pride in good works.

Dogmatism and confidence in their own sanctity have been displayed by many temperance workers. These traits have not won many converts to their position, but have actually hindered.

They have actually hardened resistance to the position they advocate, just as in another generation the belligerent pacifist was his own worst enemy.

THE CHRISTIAN ETHIC

The Christian ethic is an ethic of responsive love. Man recognizes his continuous need of the saving grace of God. He knows that the love of God was extended to him without reference to his merits. God forgave and forgives because he loves man, not because man loves God or does anything to please God. But man, whom God has forgiven, responds in love, seeking to fulfill God's will in human life. Man's response of love to God is the basis of the Christian ethic. Every deed must be judged in terms of whether it reflects man's love for God.

It is well to ask if our deeds reflect our love to God. John Wesley did not demand of any applicant for membership in the Methodist societies a pledge of abstinence from vices. He did expect, however, that as man sought God and his purposes that man would bear the fruits of the Spirit. Man would abstain from vice because he loved God and did not wish any such thing to offend God.

No man who practices abstinence for trivial reasons deserves thereby to be called Christian. The man who refrains from alcohol because he does not like the taste helps society incidentally, but is not made Christian thereby. The man who abstains to please parents is a dutiful son, but deserves no more credit. The man who will not waste his money on alcohol may be a good steward or he may be stingy; the outward deed does not indicate the motivation. The man who abstains from the use of alcohol because he believes that he can best live as God's creature without the narcotizing effect of a pleasant drug, manifests his love for God.

Man's stewardship to God relates to all that man has. This doctrine is frequently dismissed too easily as a painless way of raising the budget. Stewardship relates to man's possessions, it is true. The possessions which he holds for a season include, however, his time and his abilities as well as his money.

Every man needs to ask himself about the use of alcohol: "How best can I be a steward in relationship to alcohol? Does a moderate amount of money spent for alcohol declare me a poor steward? How much is a moderate amount? How much time can a good steward spend at a cocktail party? Does the use of alcohol as a pleasant narcotizing agent deprive me of potential which should be used for God?" These ready-made questions do not have a ready-made answer attached here. The questions are not meant as rhetorical devices; they are honest questions that should be raised by each man who is considering the use of alcohol.

The Christian ethic is concerned about one's brother and the world in which he lives. The Christian must love his brother if he is to love God. "If any one says, 'I love God,' and hates his brother, he is a liar; for he who does not love his brother whom he has seen, cannot love God whom he has not seen" (I John 4:20). Efforts must be directed toward obtaining justice for him. The Christian is concerned about the rights of his brother, although relatively unconcerned about his own rights.

Does the use of alcohol upset the workings of justice in our society? Is the use of alcohol in any way calculated to further the cause of justice? Is the insistence on the right to drink an evidence of concern for one's brother?

All too frequently any insistence on the right to drink—even moderately—is focused on the right to gratify one's own appetite. The use of alcohol may deprive the employer of his just labor, from the "half man" with a hangover to the less efficient, mildly affected moderate drinker. The use of alcohol may deprive the other person of property or life which can be lost in an automobile accident caused by a drinking driver. The use of alcohol may deprive the brother of his justice because the judgment of the drinker has been affected, and justice can no longer be distinguished from injustice.

The Christian ethic is an ethic of community. No Christian ought to plan his life apart from the company of the church. In the community of love the practice of the Golden Rule is not subtle self-seeking, but genuine self-losing. Each man is concerned with helping his brother who is weak or has a fault. Each man is willing in humility to be helped by his brother. Any sacrifice undertaken in the interest of the community is gladly assumed as part of one's response of love. Paul said of his desire to keep an ignorant brother from falling: "Therefore, if food is a cause of my brother's falling, I will never eat meat, lest I cause my brother to fall" (I Corinthians 8:13). Paul had sympathy for a man whom he knew to be wrong because of ignorance, but he was willing to become a vegetarian so that the man would remain his brother.

Every Christian is an example to other brothers in Christ. He must be most considerate of his witness to the weaker brother. It is sometimes unfortunate that the weaker brother is not always recognized as such either. There are poor examples that a Christian can set for his weaker brother; he can err either through moderate drinking or through immoderate abstinence.

The moderate drinker is often taken as an example in our society. He may go under the guise of a man of distinction. His example is powerful because his type of drinking is approved by the "best people" in society. No weak brother is apt to attempt to follow the pattern of the immoderate drinker. Rather he seeks to follow the strong man who shows that he can control alcohol. If he, through weakness, becomes an alcoholic, what of the example of the moderate drinker?

ONE IN SIXTEEN

At the present time in America at least one person out of every sixteen who drink becomes an alcoholic. Any social drinker will engage in drinking in company with many more than sixteen persons during the course of his drinking. The odds are great that one of his drinking friends will become an alcoholic. What, then, of his example?

If one out of sixteen drinkers becomes an alcoholic, how can any man know that *he* himself will not become an alcoholic? With all the uncertainty about the causes of alcoholism, can any man be sure of his abilities and powers? Or, does any Christian ever have the power to speak definitely about himself and his abilities? Is not the assertion that one will not become an alcoholic a declaration of pride and self-will? The man who is sure of his ability to continue as a moderate drinker asserts his superiority over at least 6 per cent of his brothers.

Dr. Harry Tiebout holds that the alcoholic is made well as he surrenders. Man is made whole as he surrenders to God. The total abstainer has surrendered in one area in that he expresses a lack of confidence in his ability to be a sober drinker.

The Christian ethic is contextual and concrete. It is not a set of laws, unmoved and unmoving. The Christian ethic is an expression of man's response of love to God and his fellow man worked out in a changing, sin-wracked world. The ethic is always expressed in concrete actions rather than in abstract principles. Man may follow principles accepted over the years, but he must be ready at any moment to modify his actions to the demands of the moment. The guide for all his actions is his love for God.

The Christian ethic concerning the use of alcohol must be relevant to the social and cultural situation. The high rate of incidence of alcoholism must loom large in the determination of the Christian's response to God as he considers the use of alcohol. All the other aspects of drinking patterns and habits are important too. The response of today cannot simply be derived from the answers worked out for a previous period.

Every Christian is duty bound to be informed about the problem areas concerning which decisions must be made. The Christian ought not to make ethical decisions either from ignorance or desire. He properly responds to God when he decides in knowledge and with regard to the needs of his brothers.

In a society in which the problems of drink have become so great, a radical solution may be called for. The old emphases on moderate drinking are not sufficient to prevent the rise of new problems. If every person tried moderate drinking, some would still become alcoholic. A strong recommendation by all Christian bodies for abstinence might well make substantial advances toward rehabilitation and prevention of alcoholics. It is true that such a proposal might not work either, but nothing would be lost except the gratification of an appetite for the period of the trial.

Some will object that no one has a right to ask the moderate drinker to forego his pleasure when he harms no one by the gratification. These are correct, as far as they go. This is not a discussion of rights, but of obligations and responsibilities. Man surrenders his rights in the service of God and accepts responsibilities. The appeal to abstinence is not a demand, but genuinely *an appeal* to Christians to regard their weaker brothers.

MODERN METHODISTS STILL CONCERNED

The Methodist Church has continued its interest in the elimination of the problems arising from the use of alcohol. This interest began with Wesley and arose from the situation prevailing in his day. It has continued to the present, but with various changes from time to time as the alcohol problems have shifted. Today Methodists have the most comprehensive program that has prevailed at any time.

The Methodist Church endeavors to furnish the information from which sound ethical decisions can be made. It engages in a variety of educational programs to spread knowledge throughout the church. It seeks to educate its constituents to the many varied aspects of the problem.

In Methodism education of children and youth has always been of paramount importance. Many effective methods of educating the young about alcohol are utilized. Excellent curricular materials are available. Audio-visual materials have been developed. These materials make use of the latest data drawn from scientific sources.

National youth schools on alcohol have been held. Annual conferences are encouraged to present excellent youth programs. Week-end retreats for college students discuss drinking problems as faced by young Christians. Some of the motion pictures developed by The Methodist Church are widely used in other denominations and are shown as resource materials at the Yale Summer Schools on Alcohol Studies.

The Methodist Church has always been a leader in the field of adult education. In addition to the church school materials on alcohol, it has annual regional and national schools on alcohol. These schools are held for leaders in the church, both clergy and lay. Outside authorities from the fields of medicine, social work, education, law enforcement, and other areas assist in the teaching. The women of the church have had a long-term interest in studies on alcohol. Abingdon Press has published excellent books on alcohol, such as the outstanding volumes by Clinebell and Tilson.[1]

The Methodist Church has annually had representation at the Yale Summer School of Alcohol Studies. Only one other denomination has had more ministers attend the school than have the Methodists.

The Methodist Church has accepted research as a part of education. Staff members of the Board of Temperance have read widely in the voluminous research concerning alcohol. They correlate information seeking new truths about alcohol. These findings and reports of important data are printed and distributed throughout the church in pamphlets, charts, packets, and journals.

---

[1] Howard J. Clinebell, *Understanding and Counseling the Alcoholic Through Religion and Psychology*, Nashville: Abingdon Press, 1956.
Everett Tilson, *Should Christians Drink?* Nashville: Abingdon Press, 1957.

A CHURCH-WIDE PROGRAM

The Methodist Church continues to seek justice through legislation. The legislative program is not a single-pronged attack for abolition of the liquor industry. Rather it ranges across the whole area of the provision of safeguards against the misuse of licenses, violation of fair practices, control of lobbying, control of advertising, and the regulation of the use of alcohol in connection with transportation. It is very much interested in the incidence of alcoholism as related to the prevailing form of legal control of alcohol.

The Methodist Church furnishes to its members information relative to legislation affecting alcohol. Many members write to their congressmen or state legislators concerning pending bills. The Methodist Church does not use hidden incentive nor veiled threats, but relies upon the weight of informed public opinion.

The Methodist Church has always viewed the alcohol industry as an unnecessary business. It calls for constant surveillance of the practices of the industry, especially lobbying.

The Methodist Church has adopted a strong emphasis upon rehabilitation. No longer can it be asserted truthfully that the church is uninterested in rescuing the drunkard. The church has prepared an array of excellent materials to help any local congregation work in the field of helping the alcoholic. The booklet, *Blueprint for Rehabilitation,** gives the details of a normative program. Although developed much more recently than the other phases of the program of temperance, the comprehensive program of rehabilitation is an example of the approach taken by The Methodist Church to each specific alcohol problem.

THE LOCAL CHURCH AND REHABILITATION

The usual local church program for rehabilitation will in-

* In addition to *Blueprint for Rehabilitation* the Board of Temperance has prepared action suggestions in the fields of education, commitment, and legislation. The entire set of four *Blueprints for Temperance Action* is available from that Board in a packet for 75¢ per set, 25¢ each.

clude study, discussion, analysis, and action. The study uses three well-known books in the field. The discussion follows the use of one or more films. The analysis relates to a study of the community and its facilities for assistance to the alcoholics.

The action includes education in the church on alcoholism, cooperation with the public school to secure education on a community basis, and a variety of other steps. These miscellaneous steps may on occasion seem unrelated to therapy for alcoholism, but they evidence a deep understanding of the underlying factors contributing to the development of alcoholism. The church's responsibility for the creation of community is emphasized.

Full steps for cooperation with Alcoholics Anonymous are also listed. Suggestions are also made for full cooperation with all other agencies dealing with alcoholics. In true Methodist style, if no public agencies are at work on alcoholism, the church is urged to encourage the initiation of such public progress.

Regularly conferences are being held in which ministers learn about working with alcoholics. Pastors who have acquired abilities in helping alcoholics share their knowledge and communicate their enthusiasm to others. Seminaries have taught courses to train the young minister about rehabilitation.

The success of the rehabilitation program cannot be determined at the national level, however. The General Board of Temperance of The Methodist Church has performed well in devising the program described. The program will not work unless the local church succeeds in reaching alcoholics.

A. A. is aware that the first step—the admission of the inability to control alcohol—is the most difficult. The church has no easy way of securing the admission either. The alcoholic all too frequently intends to stop drinking before he comes to the church. The church cannot afford to let him wait.

The church has problems not confronted by A. A. To many alcoholics the church seems cold and forbidding. The members appear cold and antagonistic to the fearful soul who dreads indescribable terrors. The whole history of the Methodist movement has been one of antagonism to alcohol, and it is not easy to convince alcoholics that the church is interested in them.

The church is often filled with people who do not want alcoholics in the membership. Old prejudices die hard, and not every Christian is convinced that the alcoholic is a sick person. These attitudes of resentment are expected by the alcoholic and, if discovered, furnish excuses for his next drinking bout.

Many churchmen are still unable to accept the relapses that accompany the recovery of many alcoholics. Many of them feel that conversion ought to be effective enough that it would make relapses unnecessary. An alcoholic may recover without relapse, but the congregation must never place too great a burden of expectations upon the sick drinker.

Otherwise well-intentioned church workers sometimes wish to parade the alcoholic as a badge of the righteousness of the congregation, or for some other reason. These alcoholics may deeply resent any such attempt. The alcoholic needs acceptance and may undertake leadership, but he must never feel used.

The alcoholic is often wounded by hypocritical actions he encounters in the church. Old drinking buddies (moderate drinkers, of course) may be unwilling to talk to him about drinking—or much of anything else. In many congregations drinking is not talked about openly enough for the moderate drinkers to state their views. Some of the moderate drinkers had just as soon not talk about their practices. The problems of drinking are not going to be solved until we can talk about the problem in open and frank discussion.

THE LOCAL CHURCH IN ACTION

In numerous local congregations there is little discussion of alcohol. The excellent educational materials developed to treat of alcohol are neglected. All too many church members assume that alcohol education is old style and out of date.

Every church school superintendent needs to receive reports regularly on the resources materials available from the Board of Temperance. Subscriptions to *Contact* will furnish information about the latest educational materials as well as the current programs of the church. *Contact* is a bi-weekly release of news and information published for the Boards of Temperance, World Peace, and Social and Economic Relations.

In each local church the need for social action arises. Many Methodist churches have a regularly appointed Commission on Social Concerns. Usually the Woman's Society of Christian Service is led in a program of social action by the Secretary of Christian Social Relations.

Church groups may visit the courts regularly—in which case they will see many of the fruits of the use of alcohol. They may interest themselves in clean elections—in which case they may check the closing of liquor outlets. Social action groups will certainly study pending legislation, including bills concerning the manufacture, distribution, and advertising of alcohol.

WHAT THE INDIVIDUAL CHRISTIAN CAN DO

The Methodist Church continues to call upon its members to sign vows that relate to the use of alcohol. These commitments are no longer the simple pledge which prevailed for so many years. Christians are now given a wide variety of choices by which they can show their interest in being a part of the solution rather than a part of the alcohol problem. The call to commitment is essentially an appeal to assume responsibility for one's brother, even though the responsibility can be shown in a number of ways.

The Methodist Church still holds up abstinence as the call of God for these troubled times. The program of the Church has changed and will change as the details of the alcohol problem change. It continues to regard abstinence, however, as the most logical way of solving the ethical dilemmas arising from the use of alcohol.

The Methodist Church can cooperate with other churches which do not advocate abstinence. Prominent Christian statesmen and theologians from other communions drink wine and beer regularly. These men are dedicated Christians, and The Methodist Church harms itself when it refuses to associate with them. The Methodists are not called to shut doors, but to open them.

Association with other Christians who drink moderately does not imply any lessening of the commitment to the abstinence position. It merely asserts that differences on abstinence are not great enough to make enemies of Christian brothers.

The Methodist Church believes that, although the Bible does not explicitly teach abstinence, Paul voiced a principle of regard for the weak brother that strongly suggests abstinence as the preferred reaction to alcoholic beverages. The Methodist Church is proud of Wesley's fight to bring about a spiritual and social revolution in England, including a revolution in the drinking habits of many. The Methodist Church has consistently followed the approach of social analysis of public evils as a step in the formulation of a Christian ethic. The Methodist Church has always been evangelistic to the lost, seeking out those who were uncared for by society. From these backgrounds Methodism derives its position and continues its interest in the problems arising from the use of alcohol.

INDEX

127